To Kerry x
All my love

Amanda Mead .

Trapped by the devil

KATE SPENCER

authorHOUSE®

AuthorHouse™ UK
1663 Liberty Drive
Bloomington, IN 47403 USA
www.authorhouse.co.uk
Phone: UK TFN: 0800 0148641 (Toll Free inside the UK)
       UK Local: (02) 0369 56322 (+44 20 3695 6322 from outside the UK)

Published by AuthorHouse 11/29/2021

ISBN: 978-1-6655-9502-5 (sc)
ISBN: 978-1-6655-9503-2 (e)

Trapped by The Devil – Is based on a true life story of how Kate Spencer made a decision to be financially free, but her decision to make more money quickly led her down a path that took everything from her including her freedom and her self respect.

Kate said that the one single decision she made for her to have more, led her on a soul destroying path of events for15 years. Kate says that she was **Trapped by The Devil** and was ultimatley led into the criminal underworld where she spent 13 years going in and out of prison. She suffered severe mental health issues, drug addiction, domestic abuse, emotional abuse, and uncertainty of her future. Kate found her self **Trapped** with her back against a wall and she knew that if she did not escape, she would be doomed for the rest of her life, or die a terrible death.

In 2002 after loosing both grandmother's, Kate was contemplating suicide but a power within her, urged her to find an escape and live! She found her inner strength and was able to let go of her current reality and trust the invisible force from within. Even in her darkest days, she took her attention away from the pain, suffering and destruction and she persistently listened to her intuition which led her into visualisation. She had no idea what she was doing but this one decision to trust an unseen force and surrender to the voice of her intuition, ultimately led her on a new path to freedom.

Kate took a blind leap of faith by consciously using an invisible power of imagination and intuition. Everyone had given up on her, and although she felt hopeless, she found the inner strength to keep on knocking on heaven's door. She persisted eventhough the Devil had a tight grip of her soul.

In January 2011, Kate experienced a dramatic and drastic change that would change the course of her life forever! This power of light, held her hand and helped her to divorce the Devil who had trapped her in darkness .

Visualization 2 Freedom – The secret I discovered whilst in a very dark and lonely place. I had no knowledge of the universal laws or personal growth and did this practice on intuitive impulse. Some may say that Kate was lucky as to how she self realised the hidden power of our imagination, but Kate realised that luck has nothing to do with it and that the universal laws are always working and these laws are hidden deep within everyone. Kate says that she did not realise that she was in alignment with these laws and as she persisted and applied the laws, they ultimately set her **COMPLETELY** free from a life of drug addiction, mental health disorders and crime.

WHAT OTHERS ARE SAYING ABOUT THE AUTHOR AND HER FIRST BOOK WHICH FIRST SHE WROTE IN 2012.

Amazon Reviews (https://www.amazon.co.uk)

Amazon Customer – **Wow. An inspiration to all lost souls**

> This was a most inspiring read..a young lady who could be anyone's daughter being led down a dark path of no return. Life can be change with a little faith and a willingness to try. A very personal life story with life changing affects... Great Read.
>
> - J. Bosignor.

Amazon Customer – **Brilliant**

> I know the author from school days so thought I'd read her book. I couldn't put this book down. What an amazing woman to come through this and to write such an honest and true account. Brilliant read.
>
> M. Wilmot.

Amazon Customer – **Brilliant**

> Amazing book! Knew the author from bad times to good and what an inspiration. Could not put the book down what a brilliant story :-) Keep up the good work!
>
> - H. Sutton.

Amazon Customer – **Brilliant Read**

Went to school with the author and have wondered over the years where she went or what she has been up to, she was lead down a dark path in life, but after many a year she has turned it around. Brilliant read could not put the book down read it in one night. The author is very honest and open in what's happened in her life no bars held she tells it how it is that's what makes this book a great read 10/10 for the honesty in the book.

- M. Wallace.

All reviews are honest and true and are written on https://www.amazon.co.uk

Verified google review at https://books.google.com

User review

Absolutely breath taking read. Such an inspirational woman who has truly had a rough time in life and came out the other side.

There was so many emotions flowing when reading this book you're taken on a journey of the author's life before all the wrong doing and during her darkest days, you see how easily drugs and crime can quickly turn your life upside down.

I admire this woman a great deal she now has the strength and willingness through her faith in god to help others in the same situation.

This book has filled the missing gaps that we had lost touch and I am very proud of her determination to make a better life for herself and her family. The author is now embarking on a new journey in her life. I know that with her faith in god she will be on the right paths and I intend to be there every step of the way. I thank god for saving her and bringing her back into my life.

- K. Heaven.

Social Media verified reviews (All reviewers have given written permission for their reviews to be published in this Book)

T. Thacker - So proud of you and your journey. Your book was spot on in every true life I've ever read. Thank you for being you and thank you so much for letting me read the true life events where you challenged and succeeded right to the end and the future goals you've achieved xxx

K. Collins – I read your first book, I couldn't put it down, I finished it in a few days. You are amazing for what you have over come. I'm looking forward to the new book. xx

J. Deakin – Your book was an amazing read and I'm so proud of you. I can't even imagine how hard it was for you but you have left that dark place behind and have turned into a strong woman and I admire you. Xx

M. Franks – Loved the honesty of your first book. It was written from the heart and soul. Can't wait to read your second book. Great idea for a Christmas present. X

S. Bagshaw – Loved your first book so definitely can't wait to read your next one...Looking forward to it. Xx

L. Pegg – I read your book. The inspiration you give people is real and raw. Amazing! I can't wait to buy your next book to see how you have done another 360 degree turn with your life and you have helped so many people with your life experience.

T. Wood – Your book was absolutely enthralling. Heartbreaking at times but also thoughtful. Truly inspirational to know that there is light at the end of a dark tunnel. Loved every word and couldn't put it down. Will definitely be getting the next book. xxx

J. James – I read your first book some years ago on my e-reader. It is amazing how far you have come from those dark days. The courage it must have taken to put all your past on paper and share. I look forward to reading your latest book.

A note from the Author – My new book titled "Trapped by The Devil" is a new and revised version of my first book which I wrote in 2012. Trapped by The Devil takes all the written text from the old book and has reconstructed the events to give the readers a bigger picture of what I had endured. I then bring the readers into what happened after I wrote the first book and I take them on my new journey where I was faced with a new set of challenges. In a single sentence… New level, new Devil.

All the names in this true story have been changed including the Author, but the acknowledgement of the Author's current Mentor, Emma Hague (who is a certified Proctor Gallagher Institute Consultant, business coach and mentor), does not influence the readers of this book to identify the Authors identity as Emma has many clients worldwide.

CONTENTS

BOOK 2

ACKNOWLEDGEMENTS

To my parents, who loved me and nurtured me. Mom, you kept me safe in your bosom and kick-started me into the world. Dad, you loved me as a true dad loves his daughter.

To my amazing, supportive partner, best friend, hero and soulmate. You are my rock and my main support. Thank you for loving me and for believing in me! I thank God that we have found each other.

To my son and to my amazing daughter-in-law, who are the parents to my wonderful grandchildren,

To my grandson and my granddaughter who bring me so much joy to my life, I thank God for you both. As I write this book, you both have a little sister due to arrive next year in March 2022 and I dedicate this book to her also.

To my mentor and life-coach Emma Hague, the day I saw you, I just knew you would be my business mentor and a dear friend. You are a god send. I am so very grateful for your knowledge, understanding and professionalism. Thank you Emma x (www.emmahauge.com)

To my 2 special little cousin who call me Aunty. When you both lived in the UK we spent lots of fun weekends together and the joy I experience when we meet via face-time is always amazing. Thank you both my little L&L xx..

To the team of ladies who have worked so very hard with getting my project RedFlag Well-being off the ground! You all know who you are. Every time I look at our clients, I see the foundation of love and power that we created from a single idea!

To the women I met through prison. Some of you I may never meet again and some of you are no longer with us. I wish every one of you success and love.

To the Zumba Ladies. The laughs, the parties, the fun we all had during the Zumba sessions will always be remembered. You are all amazing, beautiful souls and I am honoured to have met you all.

Finally, I have left the best until last...The Holy Spirit, the Voice of Intuition. Thank you Father for performing what can only be seen as a miracle, a sovereign touch of God upon my lost and tired soul. Thank you for enabling me to reach out to people all over the world sharing the message of hope, inspiration and salvation.

CHAPTER 1

MY CHILDHOOD

My parents were born in the West Indies and migrated to England in 1960. My mother gave birth to my brother in 1964. I was born 4 years later in 1968. In 1970, my parents moved to an area called Nechells in Birmingham UK. In 1971, my mum gave birth to my younger brother.

When I was 4 years old, I clearly recall having 2 friends that visited me every day. My friends who were called Julie and John were twins and were a little older than me. They were gentle, friendly and very kind to me and both were able to tell me events that would take place in the future. My friends never entered our home like everyone else, they could just walk through a wall, they were magical. I recall sitting with them and talking to them for hours. My parents would ask me who am I talking to and when I told them I was talking to Julie and John, they would chuckle and say; "oh, your invisible friends again". I would get a little annoyed as Julie and John were not invisible to me. I recall seeing them exactly as I saw everyone else. To me, they were real.

I recall one specific time in 1973 when my mum was pregnant. Julie and John told me that my mum was having twins, a boy and a girl. They told me that once the twins were born, I would not see them again. I was sad as I loved my special friends. Julie told me to tell my mum that she will be having twins and she asked me to tell my mum to call the boy, John and the girl Julie. I trusted my friends and I told my mum what they had said. My mum did not know that she was having twins but I recall being confident in what I was saying. I told my mum that my friends said she should call the babies John and Julie. My mum laughed but I knew she did not believe me.

In 1973, my mum gave birth to twins, a boy and a girl. My mum decided to not call the twins John and Julie, but she did give the twins names that started with the initial 'J' I recall the day that my mum gave birth to the twins, John and Julie disappeared from my life and I never saw them again.

I also have memories of being aged 4-5 years old. I can recall sitting in a chair at home on a sunny afternoon and a realisation hit me. I started looking at my hands intensely. I looked deeply at my palms and I examined my fingers and then I looked at the skin on the back of my hands and I whispered to myself; "how did I get here?" "Who am I?" "Why am I in this body?" There was a deep realisation that I was not all that I could see, I knew there was a core to my being. I intuitively knew that I was in a body, but I am not the body.

I also recall a time when I was quite young. I was sat ah home with my mum watching TV when suddenly we heard a loud flapping noise coming from our fire place. I did not know what it was but my mum knew that there was a bird stuck in our chimney. I recall my mum panicking as the noise became louder as the bird was making its way down our chimney. After a few minutes, the bird escaped the chimney and began flying around our living room. I recall the bird frantically trying to escape. Eventually, my mum managed to guide the sparrow out of one of the windows. I also recall my mum saying that a wild bird flying in someone's home is a sign of death. I did not really understand but I could feel the fear coming off my mum so I knew that she was saying it was not a good thing to experience and this disturbed me. Later on that day, we found out that a friend of my dad had died. I did not know the circumstances but I recall both of my parent's being upset and I recall growing up with this belief.

My childhood was a relatively happy experience. I spent a lot of time with my grandparents, I loved them dearly, I also spent time with my dad as we were very close. My dad is a musician and he would take me with him to some of his gigs.

When I was aged roughly between 8-9 years old, I recall being drawn to a vulnerable old lady who everyone laughed at due to the way she presented herself and with her having poor personal hygiene, some of the kids teased her by calling her smelly Nelly. This lady reminded me of the witch in Snow White and the 7 dwarfs. She was aged around 70-75 years and had a few hairs on her chin. Me and my friends used to play knock-door-run and this lady would shout at us but it made us laugh and so we would return day after day to knock on doors and run. One day, I was playing with my friends when the old lady came out of her flat carrying a steam kettle. I recall the kettle being covered with burned oil and it was not very clean. The lady was asking for someone to please help her by filling her kettle with water and boiling it for her. My friends laughed and ran away. I felt as though I was being drawn towards this woman and I felt myself walking towards her. I recall seeing the sorrow in her eyes and I reached out and took the kettle from her. My friends teased me by saying I now had germs for touching the kettle. The insults did not bother me one bit. As a young child, whenever I saw someone with a support need and knew I could help them, I would automatically be drawn to helping the person fulfil their need. As I walked home with the kettle, my friends playfully taunted me. I reached my front door and walked in to the kitchen. Both my parents were in the kitchen and when my mom saw what was in my hand she ordered me to take the dirty kettle out of her kitchen. My dad looked at me and asked me why I had a kettle. I told my parents that the old lady over the road asked for someone to boil some water for her. My dad looked at my mom and said "You should not tell a child off for doing good". My dad took the kettle off me, filled it with water and put it on the stove. Once the kettle had boiled, my dad picked it up and with his other hand he reached out for my hand and we walked together hand-in-hand to give the lady her kettle of boiling water. I recall feeling like I can somehow hear the cry of a soul in emotional pain from within other human beings.

I also spent a lot of time around my grandparents, aunts, and uncles on Dad's side of the family. I called my nan Mommy, or if I was talking about her to someone, I referred to her as Granny. I was loved so much; I did not realise this at the time but looking back, I see the sacrifices made by my grandparents and also my parents. I never really spent time with my mom's mom. I think I only saw her maybe 2-3 times a year, so I never really got to know her like I did my dad's parents. I don't have many childhood memories of visiting her. I also recall all of Mom's sisters visiting us when we lived in Nechells. I suppose it was because I was always at my other grandparent's home that I didn't see much of my mom at weekends, and she worked very hard to make our flat a home for us all during the week.

I went to mainstream school. The Junior & Infant school was at the bottom of our street and was called Cromwell Street School. I have fond memories of attending that school. I was called the teacher's pet on many occasions throughout the 7 years I attended. I recall some of the teacher's spending extra time with me and they made me feel special. In short, I would say that I was a relatively happy-go-lucky child. I had my moments where I would display challenging behaviour as most children did, but on a whole, I was loved and cared for.

A few years later, on 21 December 1980, my mom gave birth to another family addition, a beautiful baby girl. There was a twelve-year gap between the baby and me, so I naturally took on the role of the big sister and became a mother figure too. It was fun having a baby in the family since the twins were now aged 7. Our baby sister really was a beautiful child. I recall watching her sleep and leaning into her cot to kiss her chubby cheeks. I sometimes woke her up deliberately a couple of times just so I could cradle her and sing songs to her. Two years later, on 30 September 1982, another beautiful baby girl joined the family. The baby was also a beautiful child. She looked a lot like Mom, and her skin was so soft. By now I was an expert nappy changer. I made up the baby bottles, rocked the babies to sleep, told them bedtime stories, and so on. I really enjoyed helping my mom with my little sisters. Mom often went to designer stores and bought them pretty dresses, and they dressed identically too.

After the birth of the baby, we moved to an area called Stechford, as the three-bedroom flat in Nechells was too small by far to contain our family. So we moved to a five-bedroom house and I recall feeling alien in a new area. I continued to go to Duddeston Manor Secondary School in Nechells, as I'd already got settled in and my mom said that I should continue to attend that school, as I'd chosen my options for my exams.

Every morning, my younger brother and I caught the 14 bus to Nechells to go to school. I often smoked a cigarette upstairs on the bus, as it was allowed in the early 1980s. I sometimes saw a girl that also went to Duddeston Manor get on the bus about six or seven stops after me. This girl was what is known as a loner. When ever I saw her, she always looked sad. I decided to befriend her and so I would make conversation with her when she got on the bus. This young girl was bullied at school, because she had poor personal hygiene and I had heard some school kids call her fat and ugly. As a young child, I never understood bullies. I could clearly see that Jennifer always looked sad and troubled, and although my mates didn't bother with her, there was no reason why I should follow suit. Whenever I saw her on the bus, we would share a cigarette and talk about school. She wouldn't speak to me or acknowledge me whenever she saw me in school with my mates, but I always said hello to her. I did feel sorry for her, but she had this I-don't-want-to-speak-to-anyone attitude about her, I never took offence to her attitude as I sensed that this child was troubled.

My best friend at school was a girl named Jackie. We were close and became really good friends. We were both in the same maths lesson and we would whisper to each other during the lesson and so we often got into trouble by the maths teacher. The teacher was a middle aged man who wore the same blue suit almost every day. We could identify that he drank alcohol and smoked cigarettes as the signs were there for all to see. He'd swear at us if he was in a bad mood. You could smell tobacco and alcohol on his breath and his teeth were discoloured. If he was in a bad mood and you answered the questions to your work correctly, he would put big crosses next to your answers. However, if he was in a good mood, he'd give you big ticks and write "bloody marvellous" in big red letters on your page. Even if your answers were incorrect, he would still tick the work and give you a big smile! I recall being in his class one day, and it was about fifteen minutes to the end of school. The fire alarm was ringing, and he ran and locked the classroom door with all of us inside. When someone shouted, "Sir, it's a fire drill and we have to evacuate the premises," he told that person to shut up and remain seated as he believed it was not a fire bell but the end-of–school bell but no one was leaving until we had all finished our work! When he eventually realised he was in the wrong, he mumbled an apology and opened the classroom door for us to leave for the day. I look back at the school days and recall being impatient with life. I went through the stages of dreaming of being 16, and then 18 years old and not having to be told to attend school. If I had a crystal ball to see into the trials and challenges that lay waiting for me, I think I would have embraced every moment of every day as a young child.

I also recall a time when I was in my computer studies class and the teacher who taught us about computers had quite a broad Birmingham accent. His name was Mr Parker. One day as Mr. Parker was sat at his desk, we were supposed to be working on our computers. In our class was a group of boys who were always messing around and playing tricks on us girls, but one or two of them were quite serious most of the time and this made us girls laugh because in our opinion, the Mr. Serious act just did not fit them well. I was sat next to a girl named Monica. As we sat and talked, we both noticed that one of the boys in the class had taken his beret cap off and placed it on a table which was close to Monica and I. Monica and I both looked at the beret cap and it was as if we both had a devilish thought at the same time. Without a word, Monica sneaked over to the table and picked up his beret cap. Monica passed it to me. We had scissors on our desk that day and I reached for them and I cut the beret off the cap. It was such a spontaneous action. I had not given this action any thought. Monica and I couldn't stop laughing. After a little while, we noticed that the owner of the beret cap was looking around the classroom for his cap. When he couldn't find his cap, I recall him looking puzzled but he returned to his seat. Once he was sat down at his desk, I noticed a roll of thick parcel sellotape near to our desk. I decided to stick the beret back on the cap using this thick brown tape and we put the beret where it would not be obvious that we were the ones who had taken it. When this lad found his cap and saw that the beret had been cut off and stuck back on with brown tape, he went crazy. To this day I do not believe we ever owned up!

CHAPTER 2

BEING A GREEN TEEN

As time passed, I became a young and vibrant teenager. I went out clubbing every weekend to the clubs and wine bars in the city centre. I would return home in the early hours of the morning and wake the whole house up as I could never find my front door key. I remember Christmas Eve just a few weeks after we moved to Stechford. As I still went to Nechells every weekday to attend school, I had not really made an effort to make new friends in Stechford and so I remained close to my school mates. We were loud and always played practical jokes on other pupils in our school. None of us really had any time for boyfriends; we thrived on girl power. I was thirteen years old, and I went to a blues party with a mate who was a year younger than me. When it was over, it was early hours on Christmas Day, and everyone knows that there is not any public transport on Christmas Day. So, I ended up staying over at my mate's, house because I was tired and had no means of transportation to get home. I woke up late in the afternoon on Christmas Day and had to brave facing my parents and the long, cold lonely walk from Nechells to Stechford, as I did not know any short cuts I followed the bus route which took around an hour from Nechells to Stechford. I got home in the early evening. I did not know what all the fuss and upset was about. My parents and my siblings were distraught; the turkey had not met the oven. My parents looked as if they'd been on a crash diet, and all eyes were on me as if they'd just seen a ghost! My dad never used to smack us as kids; that was Mom's job, but on this day, he made an exception. In the past, he had only to give us that look—you know the one where the eyes would do the shouting? Yeah, that one, but that day I felt my Christmas present! The way I screamed the house down, I'm surprised our neighbours didn't dial 999 for the police. I'm sure everyone who heard me really thought I was going to die from the way I carried on! But saying all of that, I was a real drama queen with a capital Q. That was just one incident I recall when I was a teenager.

I used to meet up with my friends from School almost every Saturday afternoon. This soon changed when I began working full-time in retail. In the late 1980's, there was a government funded scheme called a Youth Training Scheme (YTS). I worked in retail selling High Street fashion clothes, and on Saturdays the manager allowed me to wear the latest fashions to promote the highly priced stock. The manager was very kind to me and so it provoked envy with a couple of the other women that worked there. I could see that some of the other staff didn't like the fact that I was allowed that privilege to wear some of the latest fashion and some were quite vocal about it, and what made matters worse was the fact that the manager was quite strict with the other women but she was very kind to me and I often saw her warm heart. I would ignore their stares and remarks. Some of the women who worked at the fashion store were lovely and always supported me in my new role as sales assistant. After about 6 months I left that placement and worked in a shoe shop, but after a few weeks I was offered a part time position working in a high end shoe store. Whilst working part time, I met two really nice ladies and we became close friends. All the staff at this shoe store were pleasant and I really enjoyed working as part of a team. The two women who I got on really well with also worked part time and some evenings after work, we would go to the pub and sometimes we would meet up some weekends.

It was 1985 and I was sixteen years old when I had the weirdest dream ever. I don't recall how the dream started, but I can clearly recall what the dream was about. I was walking on a golden beach looking at the calm sea which was the most beautiful shade of blue I've ever seen. The sky was just as beautiful, as was the bright sun. I was with a stranger and he was a picture of perfection and he was peaceful. He had a sense of perfection and He was an immaculate being. We were walking on the beach, and we talked. Here is the mystery: when he spoke to me, a foreign language came out of his mouth, a language I'd never heard before in my life, but

I understood every word that He uttered. What was even weirder was when I talked to Him, the same foreign language came flowing out of my mouth, but I knew what I was saying. One thing I will say is that it was the most peaceful dream I have ever had in my life. It was such a calm, tranquil dream, and I was so peaceful. At no point was I afraid, and when I woke up, I was extremely happy inside but had no idea why! I mentioned the dream to a couple of people to hear what they thought, as it was a mysterious dream, but no one could tell me what it meant. I don't know why, but I thought it was God. I say I don't know why but when I articulate the dream I know without a shadow of doubt that I was in the presence of God. It was an intuitive feeling. I recall feeling peace, joy, love and acceptance. When I mentioned it to a family friend who is religious (Seventh Day Adventist), she told me it wasn't God because no one has seen Him. I also mentioned it to a mate who'd recently converted to Islam, and he said the same—that it wasn't God, as no one has ever seen God. So, who was this man in my dream, the perfect stranger? I just thought I'd share that dream with you, as it has always been in the mists of my mind. I also had a vision one day whilst I sat in a maths class. I was kind of daydreaming to begin with, and then I had a vision of the sun beating down on the earth, the sky bright and blue, and then there was a crack of thunder and the sky turned pitch black. I mentioned this to a few people, and one person told me that what I had seen was an eclipse. It was *not* an eclipse that I saw. The sky didn't just darken; it was as if it was midday one minute and then midnight the next. I saw a lot of strange spiritual things growing up and I just thought I would share some of these mystical moments with you all.

Also, when I was seventeen years old, I met a girl who became my best mate. She lived just over the road from our house. My friend, her mom and her siblings had recently moved into the area from a place called Tamworth. My friend was a competitive disco dancer. She entered dance competitions all over the country and had joined a local dance studio in the area. One Saturday morning, she asked me to meet her at the dance studio she'd recently joined. She had stayed over at her nan's house in an area called Shard End just outside of Stechford, where we lived. She arranged to meet with me at the studio, so I made my way there to meet with her. I waited until the class had finished, but she didn't show up. I

9

struck up a conversation with one of the teachers at the studio who taught ballroom dancing, and out of the blue he asked if I wanted a job in the studio. He knew I wasn't a disco dancer, as I'd explained this to him during our conversation about why I was there. So, when he asked if I wanted a job, I initially thought it was a cleaning job or helping in the café. When he offered me the job as teaching dancing, I didn't really understand what he was saying to me. I explained that this was the first time I'd ever been in a dance studio as I wasn't into disco dancing and never really had any knowledge of what it was all about. He said that my mate was going to be working on a Youth Training Scheme from Monday morning and there was room for me to learn what the position entailed. In the meantime, he wanted me to start as soon as possible. I agreed without really knowing what I was agreeing to. He then took me into a smaller studio and said that I could start by taking a private lesson with one of the pupils who was also a competitive dancer. Basically, I was thrown in the deep end and didn't really have a clue, but I got on with it and found it really easy to do. I have always loved to dance and so In the next six months, I was trained up to conduct my own keep-fit class, and as the current world champion disco dancers had joined the studio to teach, I learned from them. I took intense dance lessons to learn the moves and how to teach them. After I'd been teaching dance for a while, I got a job with a lot more responsibilities and a much healthier income in a place called Dudley in the West Midlands. After a short time in the dance studio in Dudley, I took my official exam to be a semi-pro teacher, and six months after that I took my final exam and became a qualified professional dance instructor. I also went to competitions with my dancers and was asked to be an adjudicator at some of the venues.

Most weekends I would go out clubbing with my mates. As time went by, I became close to another girl who was two years younger than me named Laura. We became good friends. Every Saturday night, we went to a club called Tabasco's which was in an area called Witton in Birmingham not far from the city centre. We had some laughs in that club. When ever we went out, we would always return home together no matter what.

In March 1988 my granddad was diagnosed with cancer of the bowls and he was at Dudley Road Hospital. I use to pass the hospital on my way to work but I never once visited him when he was there. I recall thinking that he would soon be home and I could visit him then as I did not really like going into hospitals. The last time I saw my granddad was in a pub called the White Swan on Victoria Road, Aston. He was telling someone that I was his first granddaughter. I remember thinking he'd got it wrong and saying to him, "I'm your second grandchild," as I've got an older brother. But he corrected me and said, "No, you're my first granddaughter. My first grandchild is your brother." He was admitted to hospital shortly after I saw him in the pub. A few weeks later, my mom received a phone call from the hospital letting her know that her dad had passed away. That was the first death in the family, and it was my granddad, and his birthday was May 1, and he died a couple of days before that. A short while after he died, I dreamed that God asked me what I wanted. I just remember a voice in the sky. I said, "Lord, my granddad has died, and I never saw him before he went. Can I see him, please?" I recall seeing a beautiful blue sky with the sound of birds singing sweetly, and there he was, my granddad, smiling just like he used to when telling someone that I was his first granddaughter. He was smiling down from the clouds at me. He looked happy. Suddenly, there was a loud crack of thunder, and it went pitch black and I saw him no more. I thanked God for showing me my late granddad as I felt some peace and I believed he was OK.

After that dream, I found peace in my life concerning the loss of granddad. The guilt I felt before having that dream was unbearable. I knew there was a God and I believed that He was from above. I just didn't understand anything about Him. My mom told us as children about judgement day, and I used to visualize the whole world standing before God and Him asking us questions like, "Why did you do this wrong and that wrong whilst you were on earth?" It was too scary to think about as a child, so I tried not to think too much about judgement day. I also recall my mum telling me about the end of the world. I could not get my head around what my mum told me. I use to sit and question what she had said as I realised that when I die, how will I know for certain that everyone else had died? Also, if everyone else died and I was alive to witness it then that's not the end of the world as I would still be alive? I didn't say anything to my mum about her statement but I did ponder on the idea in my mind.

In 1988, I started dating a guy called Simon. Because I was a dance instructor, I had not made any plans on becoming a parent or having any children, as I wasn't parental and wanted to keep my flat tummy and all my curves. Although I enjoyed playing mum to my younger sisters, I liked the fact that I could hand them back to my mom when the going got tough. Children are lovely but I just was not paternal.

In April 1989, I found I was pregnant. When I was only a few weeks into the pregnancy, I didn't want Simon anywhere near me! I don't know what it was, but I didn't like him very much when I was pregnant. Not very nice, I know, but sometimes that's hormones for you!

HOW TO BOOK A DISCOVERY CALL WITH THE AUTHOR

#mentorship/help/support – Are you experiencing challenges with your teenage son or daughter? Can you relate to chapter 1? Book a discovery call by contacting me at info@redflagwellbeing.co.uk

CHAPTER 3

FIRST ENCOUNTER WITH THE LAW

On 3 February 1990, I gave birth to a beautiful baby boy. I found being a new mom quite exciting and enjoyable. I fell into the role of a loving proactive mom considering I didn't think I was paternal. I took to being a new mom like a duck to water. I christened Josh when he was five months old. I tried to get a hall booked for 29 July 1990, as that's my older brother's birthday and I felt it would be nice to have a double celebration. However, that date was unavailable, so I opted for the week before and we celebrated Josh's Christening on the 22nd July 1990. My grandparents loved Josh dearly, as he was the first great-grandson, and he was a comical baby. He never really cried, but when he did, he sounded like a little lamb, he was so cute, now let's move on.

On the 8th July of 1991, I decided to go to a community centre to attend a keep-fit class. I knew most of the staff at the centre as I taught keep-fit and held dance classes there for children in the 1980's. I arrived at the community centre half an hour before the class was scheduled to start so a member of staff handed me the keys to the hall and told me I could wait in there until the keep-fit instructor arrived. I let myself into the hall and decided to warm up with a few gentle stretches whilst I waited. As I warmed up, I saw something out of the corner of my eye moving. It was a sparrow trapped in the room. I noticed that a window was open but the bird kept flying around in circles but not going near the opened window.

As the sparrow started flying around the hall I panicked. I remembered the incident of a wild bird being in our home when I was little and the memory of my mothers words hit my heart. I recall being very anxious and so I decided to leave the hall and wait outside for the instructor and other ladies to arrive. After what seemed like a lifetime, the keep-fit instructor arrived with two ladies. I was relieved and I gave her the keys. I was hoping that the bird may have flown out of the opened window but when we all stepped in to the hall, it was still frantically flying around the room. The keep-fit instructor was very calm and guided the bird out of the window. We started the class and I could not concentrate as I kept thinking that someone had died or someone was about to die. I could not get the thought out of my head. I made my way home, cooked a meal and settled down to eat and watch TV. My dad was sat in an armchair and decided to go out. As my dad closed the front door, our telephone started ringing. My mom was upstairs and answered the phone. After a few seconds, my mom started calling my dad. I answered her and told her that he had just gone out. My mom sounded nervous and said that someone should go out and call him back as it was my granny calling to say that she thinks Papa had died. As soon as I had heard those words, I remembered the sparrow. I felt numb and I placed my cutlery down on the table. I recall running upstairs to my mom and shouting at her saying HOW CAN GRANNY "THINK" THAT PAPA IS DEAD? The rest of the evening was a bit of a blur but the bottom line was that my grandad had died. One of my brothers had managed to catch up with my dad and they both returned. My dad spoke to Granny over the phone and when he hung up, he told us all to get in his car as we were going to Granny's. When we arrived, all of my aunts, uncles, cousins and family friends were comforting each other. My grandmother told us that Papa was intoxicated last week and fell over and bumped his head off their marble fireplace. She said that as he often fell over when he was drunk, no one assumed anything would come of it. Papa would also spend 3-4 days in bed with headaches and dehydration due to the excessive amount of alcohol consumption so when he complained of having a headache it was assumed that he was hung over. Papa died of a blood clot to his brain. Papa's funeral was held on July 22nd 1991 – One year after Josh's Christening. On 22nd July 1990 we got together as a family to celebrate a life, 12 months on 22nd July 1991 we gathered together again but this time it was to say goodbye to Papa.

Josh was a good baby until he hit age two! I continued to teach dance classes and on most occasions, I took my son with me to the classes, and what a challenge that was! But it was worth it, as he was a happy and contented child. I only taught dancing part-time after school hours. My clients included all ages, from children to adults, so I also worked part-time jobs in the mornings and early afternoons. From 1992 to 1995, I worked in a well-known betting shop as an assistant manager and watched as some of the customers threw their money down the drain. Don't get me wrong; I saw a few people win, but I also saw a lot more lose! Later in 1995, I decided to work in our local post office. I enjoyed working as a post-office cashier, and the transactions were quite interesting. In April, I met a man who I started dating. He was flash and appeared to be wealthy. At first, I would say that I was not physically attracted to him but he had a lovely personality. As the weeks passed, he grew on me and I began to like him a lot. I had alarm bells ringing in my head as something did not quite sit right but I chose to ignore the bells and put it down to me being silly.

Because I had started my new job very near to Christmas that year, I hardly had any money. Looking back, it really didn't matter, because we all had a lovely Christmas, and no one went without a huge dinner and presents. I recall visualizing having lots of money and the feeling would excite me as I imagined buying my loved ones all the things they wanted. Night after night I would see, smell and touch the money and the lifestyle I wanted in my imagination, so when I was approached by someone to commit fraud, it didn't take too much persuading, especially considering the amount of money that was involved. I feel that I need to make you aware that I did not have a goal how to earn more money, I just kept on visualizing about having huge amounts of money and what I could do, be, and have. I started off with smaller amounts; £6,000.00 was the first amount I stole. Then, it quickly escalated to £10,000 and £15,000.00. After a few weeks, I was taking £45,000.00 on an average day. In May I decided to rent a 3 bedroom house a few doors away from my parents house. By now I had a ridiculous amount of designer clothes, different wigs, handbags, expensive jewellery and my new home was fully furnished with beautiful expensive furniture. I brought a black Ford Cabriolet convertible car which I loved. I also brought gifts for my family and friends. Tony and I decided to take my son and youngest sister on a short holiday to Blackpool

Pleasure Beach. My friend Laura joined us with her partner and her 2 little girls. We stayed in a B&B not too far from the pleasure beach and the children loved it there. Whilst in Blackpool one day, I decided to go on a ride which was called the cat & mouse. Here I was, dressed like I was going to a party with my designer clothing on and so deciding to go on a ride was not one of my best ideas. Tony and I sat in the carriage of the cat & mouse ride and we were strapped in by one of the men who worked on the rides. I had decided to wear a wig that day, like I said earlier, not my best idea to go on a fairground ride. Tony and I sat waiting for the ride to begin. Without any warning, we were jolted forward as the ride began. As we were swung around a bend, I noticed that my head felt cold. I touched my head to find that my wig had come off my head and the person who sat behind us had my wig glued to his face! I was frantically attempting to grab my wig off the man who sat behind me but the ride was throwing us around and I was not able to grasp my wig. At some point I managed to grab my wig but with the ride throwing us around, I could not get my wig on. Eventually, the ride slowed down and I quickly placed my wig on my head. I realised that I had put my wig on lopsided as the fringe was on my ear. I impatiently adjusted my wig and faced the embarrassing stares of others. I look back and laugh at this moment because as frustrating and embarrassing this moment was, it was also hilarious too. On the whole, we had a lovely break for 3 days in Blackpool and the kids really enjoyed themselves. When I returned back to Birmingham and back to work, I continued to steal from the post office as it had become my new way of life and I hated it and I told myself that I will stop doing this next week. Some days I'd take about £20,000.00 in the morning and then another £40,000.00 in the afternoon. This went on for six months. The post-office staff didn't suspect what I was doing, in fact, no one did. It was Tony (the man I was dating at the time) who led the police to me through his stupidity. He was bragging in a casino one night, and the staff contacted the police as they suspected that he was committing some sort of crime due to the large amounts of money he flashed around. He was also heavily involved in the post office scam. All of my family and friends thought that I'd bagged myself a wealthy man because of the amount of cash I had in my possession. I didn't tell anyone what I was doing, but I couldn't look my Granny in the eye, as I felt guilt grip me. The amount of money

I took out of the post office was scandalous. If you think 6-7 figures, then you'll have an idea! It all came to an end on the 16th December 1996. I was arrested and charged with conspiracy to steal. Then, after I appeared in court, the charge was dropped to theft from employer. I had several court appearances from December 1996 through May 1997. It was May 1997 when I received an eighteen-month custodial sentence and was sent to HMP Brockhill, Redditch. However, it was my first time to be in front of the courts, and I didn't have a previous criminal record. I also had a very good solicitor. As a result, out of the eighteen months, I had to serve nine months. The police and courts didn't confiscate a penny from me even though they had seen documentation and goods that I had acquired with the stolen cash. The police had seen all my household items, clothes, car, and jewellery, as well as the cash receipts to prove I'd been a very busy lady indeed, but they left me with all the possessions I had acquired through my criminal activities! I admitted the offence in police interview, as I was caught bang to rights. The judge told me that although I was a nice lady with a previous good character, he had no choice but to give me a custodial prison sentence as this was a serious offence. During the police raid, the police had recovered a Christmas list which showed that I was planning to spend a lot of the money on my immediate family. The police also found receipts and documentation which showed that I spent a few thousand pounds on people who were needy and who did not have much. All the clothes I owned were designer clothes. The amount of clothes and cosmetics I owned, I could have easily opened a huge shop! Having all of these possessions made me very miserable. It felt like I was empty inside and I was looking for a way to fill a void within. Looking back, I would describe my feelings as emotional pain.

I started my sentence in a closed prison, HMP Brockhill, Redditch. I recall walking through the prison gates in handcuffs escorted by a Group 4 officer from Birmingham Crown Court. I arrived in the reception area, where I was asked a series of questions regarding my next of kin, home address, and so forth, as well as a lot of security questions. I was also strip–searched, as this procedure is a must for everyone who walks through the prison gates from court. The officers were quite friendly as they introduced themselves and explained prison life to me. Leading up to the court case, the thought of prison petrified me but once I was actually there, the fear had gone. This was my new home for nine months, and I could either allow it to break me and consequently spend the time the hard way or get on with it knowing that I was not going anywhere, and reminding myself that I have a release date. I had to make the best out of a bad situation. After the reception department, I was led to the induction wing, which was D wing, and was put in a dormitory with three other inmates. As soon as I walked in, I saw the faces of three ordinary women who, like me, had broken the law. I immediately warmed to them and they to me. One of the women in the cell was pregnant and was talking of having a visit with someone who she hoped would bring her drugs. I used to judge people for being careless with their children, but look what I had done, and I had no excuse apart from the love of money. Greed is a terrible thing. We had a toilet in our cell, and we ate our meals around a dining table situated by the staff office. I was only on D wing for a couple of days and then I was transferred to the main side of the prison. I believe I was moved over only after a few days as I did not present as high risk, having no thoughts to self harm, no suicidal risks or challenging behaviours. Some women are extremely vulnerable in prison and very timid. I would spend time speaking with the most vulnerable prisoners and do my best to give them hope. I had always been confident and very rare was I overwhelmed with some of life's challenges and I never looked at prison as a place where I felt threatened. And so, I was moved to C wing on the main side of the prison, where I was put in a single cell. In the cell was a single bed nailed to the hard, cold floor; a mini wardrobe with a chest of drawers attached; and a metal desk where I sat to eat my meals and write my letters to my family and friends who were in the outside world. There was a toilet in the recess area, as we didn't have toilets in the cells on the main side. I made the cell my home, as it was where I had to live for the next few months and it was the place where lay my head at night. I met a lot of women there to whom I got quite close. As I was a female MC and I wrote all my own lyrics, I used to entertain some of the girls during association time. Most of the women I spoke to in prison were addicted to heroin, crack cocaine or both. That was the first time I ever saw heroin in my life. I always thought that heroin had to be injected into the vein but I witnessed someone smoking it on foil. I told myself that there was no way I was going down that road; I didn't really understand what made people want to destroy themselves and wasn't shy in voicing my opinion. I was of the opinion that anyone who took drugs were weak and I could not see myself ever taking any form of drug whatsoever. Based on the memories I hold of that prison sentence, I'm quite confident that I can write a book on what it's really like behind prison walls. After being on C wing for 6 weeks, I remember being in my cell after lunch when an officer unlocked my door and told me to pack my things, as I was to be shipped out to an open prison. I didn't want to leave the girls I'd met, as we had become close. There were tears and broken hearts as we said our good-byes. I wasn't alone on the ship-out; there were another five or six girls going to HMP Drakehall with me. I recall being sad and happy at the same time. Sad to say goodbye to some really lovely women who I had grown to know and like, but also happy to close one chapter on my prison journey and move on to a prison with less restrictions and a lot of fresh air.

We arrived at the open prison, and it was very different from a closed jail. It looked like a little village. There was a farm on the prison grounds where some of the inmates had been given the job of looking after chickens. Once we settled in and were shown our rooms—not cells—it not only looked like a village but was like living in one too. Some of the other women serving prison sentences didn't look like your average criminals, if you get my drift, and others you could tell had been in and out of prison for years. As time went by, I found myself adapting to prison life, as this open jail held no real punishment. Yes, I had been sent to prison, locked away from the outside world, friends, and family, but once I had served two-thirds of my sentence, I was eligible for town visits and home leave. My family visited me every single week without fail until I was allowed to visit them. My dad would then drive down to the prison to pick me up in the morning, and I had to be back by a certain time. I remember coming back from one town visit. I was on time (according to my watch); however, my personal officer was working in the reception department that day and according to her watch, I was late returning. Not only was I late according to the officer's watch and the clock on the prison gate, but I'd had a drink of wine whilst I was off the prison premises and was slightly tipsy too. My personal officer Mrs M.,informed me that I was two minutes late according to her watch and consequently I would appear in front of the prison governor on Monday morning. She didn't mention the smell of alcohol on my breath or say anything about me presenting as slightly intoxicated; she totally ignored my unstable stance. I protested and stood firm, as my watch was telling me that I was on time. I was served an adjudication sheet (also known as a nicking sheet), and I was in front of the governor Monday morning. The governor was known for giving out extra days for sneezing at the wrong time! I wasn't fazed by her, as I knew I was right in my defence. Monday morning arrived and I appeared before the governor, my personal officer and another prison officer. After reading the comments written on the nicking sheet and reading the report that said I had been late retuning to the prison, the governor asked the two staff members and me to tell her the time on our watches. She also told the time on her watch, and all four of us had different times. After that, the governor decided that there was no case against me and that there was to be a new rule that everyone who left the prison for rehabilitation, whether a town visit or home leave, must go by the clock at the prison's main gate. That rule is still in place today. I was also home for Christmas that year. I was granted home leave and was able to spend five days with my family and friends. Laura and I went to see a Jamaican artist at the Aston Villa Leisure Centre, and I bumped into one of the prison officers from the prison I was currently at. We looked at each other and said our awkward hellos, but I don't know who was more shocked, me or her! That's just one of the many little stories I wanted to share with you to give you an insight into prison life back in 1997.

CHAPTER 4

THE PRINCE OF DARKNESS

Whilst serving my sentence in the open prison, I received a letter from someone from a prison over in London. The person who wrote to me was named Darren and he knew all about me, as he'd said that he had heard about the scam with the post office from someone who was also in prison. Out of curiosity, I replied to Darren, as I was interested in how he had come across my name. I was also very naive and vulnerable but didn't know that at the time. In fact, if someone would have told me how vulnerable I was, I would not have understood and quite possibly, I would have been annoyed. The crime I'd committed was spoken of with admiration in the criminal underworld, and that's how Darren had heard about me. Soon I was in regular contact with Darren. If I recall correctly, I would say we became pen-pals after his first letter to me. It was not long before letters were going to and fro between us, and before I knew it, we had gone from pen pals to lovers through the post! Because there's a lot of jail mail in which women write to men they've met in jail and vice versa, it seemed pretty normal to find a man through the power of the pen. I suppose I became infatuated with this man. I really wanted something that I couldn't have, and that was the attraction if I'm perfectly honest. It wasn't long before we were having inter-prison phone calls too. I loved the smooth cockney accent and I was swept off my feet by his Southeast London twang. Looking back it was very Silly of me to have allowed a complete stranger who I had only met on paper, draw me in. This communication between us, continued until when I was released in February 1998, I continued to stay in touch with him through letters and visits. When Darren first contacted me, he was in a prison called HMP Belmarsh. After a few weeks into our "pen-pal" relationship, Darren had been moved to another prison which was on the Isle of Wight, HMP Camphill. I'd been to visit Darren at HMP Camphill a few times. I told my parents about Darren and I recall my mom not being happy as she said that I deserved better. I recall being angry with my mom and I thought she was being judgemental. I refused to listen to anyone who advised me to run for the hills from Darren. Could they see something I was too blind to see? Was I listening to my emotions and ignoring my gut feeling? Since being released from prison, I got a 2 bedroom property from Birmingham City council. One night I was sat at home when the phone rang. It was Darren calling me from HMP Camphill. He was sobbing like a little baby, as he'd just been told by the prison Chaplain that one of his older sisters had been found dead on his birthday. Darren told me that he was in shock and he needed me to book a visit to see him. I recall feeling really sad for him and I felt that it must be hard hearing of a family death whilst in prison. Darren also asked me to attend his sisters funeral as soon as a date had been confirmed. He practically begged me to be there for him at the funeral in London and I told him I would be there although I felt that I wasn't ready to meet the rest of Darren's family and under such circumstances, it was not the ideal way I had imagined I would be meeting my boyfriends family. I felt I was backed into a corner, but what else could I do? Once a funeral date was established, I attended Darren's sisters funeral. When I arrived, I met Darren's family. Darren arrived shortly afterwards and he was handcuffed and escorted by two prison officers; he was handcuffed to one of the officers.

Darren's sister had passed away on his birthday in May. Darren was released from prison on the 16th December 1998. I travelled down to London on a coach on the morning of his release. I went down to London to meet him. (He'd been moved from the Isle of Wight back to HMP Belmarsh, London.) The day Darren got out of jail; I saw him do drugs. The first time I'd seen heroin was in HMP Brockhill. I saw an inmate doing heroin in her cell. I later heard that she was "chasing the dragon"—smoking heroin on a piece of tinfoil. It looked horrible and it stunk of cat wee! I also remember looking at this woman and clearly seeing the devil himself looking back at me through her eyes! I remembered that look and Darren had the same evil look in his eyes. This led to us having a big argument in the middle of the street, and he threatened me with all sorts of things. Don't get me wrong; I gave as good as I got, as I can be a feisty character when the fancy takes me. I just did not understand. Darren had never disclosed that he had taken drugs in the time I had known him and I was not aware of the signs of an addict apart from the look I saw in the female inmates eyes when I witnessed her taking drugs in prison. Darren told me that he was not a drug user and that he was not addicted. He said he was still grieving from the loss of his sister and he said he heard that heroin would take some of the grief away. Darren swore to me that he was not addicted and he was really sorry for taking heroin. I believed him. The fight between Darren and I ended as quickly as it had started. Eventually we were on the coach leaving London heading toward Birmingham to my two-bedroom flat. He'd sworn to me that he had only taken heroin that one time as a stress relief, having just come out of jail and that he wouldn't do it again, especially with what had happened to his sister, and like a prize mug, I really believed him!

My son was now seven years old, but he couldn't get used to living away from his nan and granddad, who lived down the road from our 2 bedroom flat. My son made it clear that he didn't like my new partner, and I put it down to him wanting his mom all to himself. I also knew Josh blamed Tony, my ex-partner, for us being separated when I was in prison, as Tony was also involved in the post-office fraud. My whole family blamed Tony for leading me astray. In reality, I held all the cards and wasn't the sweet little innocent post office clerk they made me out to be!

Consequently, Josh was always at my mom and dad's house, which meant that Darren and I spent a lot of time together alone in the flat. He'd only been out of jail and in my flat for about two weeks before the emotional abuse and domestic abuse started. The funny thing is that I knew a few women who were victims of domestic abuse, and I had always sworn that no man would ever treat me like that, as I wouldn't stand for it. I also thought that with all the hot-blooded males in my family, no man would ever get the chance to abuse me. But when it happens to you, you do not see what is staring you in the face as you could be soul-tied (which

23

is also called co-dependency) to that person and emotionally involved, so you aren't looking at the situation with a clear seeing as you do when it is somebody else going through the mess. It was as if I was practically wearing bifocal specs and still suffering short sightedness! It didn't take Darren long to mentally break me down either, as he began with mental torment, emotional abuse, which progressed to the physical violence.

I became quite timid in the matter of a few days. It seems quite ironic, really, but the truth is that men like Darren have a game plan, and that is to destroy, destroy a bit more, and then completely destroy. He was a complete control freak. I can recall one night out, we went into my dad's regular pub, called The Rock Pub, to have a drink. Earlier that night, Darren had backhanded me in the mouth, and my lip was slightly swollen. When my dad saw me, he could see the sorrow in my eyes, and I knew he didn't notice my lip, as it was only slightly swollen. My dad spoke to me in his caring way that only my siblings and I ever see. My dad asked me if I was OK? I lied and put a brave face on and said that I was fine. My dad had always said that he would go to prison for any of his children if anyone hurt us and that was running through my mind. My dad also didn't like Darren either. Come to think of it, none of my immediate family liked him, but because he was my boyfriend, they bit their lip and just observed our relationship for my sake. If only I had been brave enough to open my mouth and tell someone what had happened, but I wasn't.

Darren travelled to and from London on a regular basis to see his probation officer and his friends. He was also in receipt of benefits from DWP and his benefits office was based in London. Darren told me he would continue to claim his benefits from the benefits office which was in Woolwich Arsenal, London. I began working as an area manager for a large cleaning company and enjoyed my job. It didn't bother me that I was working, and Darren wasn't, as I realised, he was not long out of prison and required time to rehabilitate back into the community as best he could. When Darren had to visit the benefits office every 2 weeks, I sometimes travelled down to London with him.

Not long after Josh turned eight, we all travelled down to London to spend the weekend there and to meet Darren's dad. Darren and I stayed in a bedroom at his dad's flat, and we made up a sofa bed for Josh to sleep on in the living room where he seemed comfy as Josh also had his game console and the TV. I met Darren's dad and he seemed like a nice man, but he and Darren had a massive argument, and this resulted in his dad leaving and saying to Darren, "It's only because there is a lady and a child with you that I haven't thrown you out of my home!" With that his dad left, and we planned to leave Sunday afternoon so that I could return to work on Monday morning so that Josh could go to school.

It was late Friday night, and Josh was asleep in the living-room on the sofa bed while Darren and I sat in the bedroom listening to music. Darren began to get some tinfoil out and smooth any creases, he flashed a lighter flame over the foil, and made a tube. I was mortified watching him, as he performed this action like a real professional. When I asked him what he was doing, he looked at me and said, "I'm making a plate and tube. Why?" He answered me as if I was stupid! I was absolutely gobsmacked! I watched as he placed the brown powder on the foil plate, light a flame and smoke the heroin. I really cannot find the words to describe the emotions that ran through my body as I watched him do drugs. I was then forced to take heroin. When I say forced, I mean that he told me for about two hours to just trust him and do it. He threatened me with beatings, which was the easiest of the torments. From what I can remember, he didn't hit me that much; because he'd hit me in the past, the fear of it happening again was terrifying for me, and all he had to do was threaten. The fact that my son was in the other room did bother me, as I didn't want my Josh to hear his mom being traumatised and beaten. When Darren saw I wouldn't be moved, he went straight for the ultimate kill. He threatened to beat my son to a pulp; he knew my boy was my weakest link. After he said that he'd beat my eight-year-old son, fear gripped me by the throat. All this happened in his dad's flat on the Old Kent Road in London. If we'd been in Birmingham, I suppose I would have stood a chance, but with no one to run to in a strange place, I felt I didn't really have a choice. We were on the second floor of a small block of flats alone with something like twelve locks on the front door, and I wasn't going to jump out of a window, although at the time I felt that if my son hadn't been with me, I'd have taken a chance, as anything is better than being trapped by the devil himself. This man claimed he loved me and couldn't understand why I wouldn't make this little sacrifice for him! "All I want you to have is a couple of lines, babe. Just trust me. You'll be fine." I will not say what actual threats he made or the things he said he'd do to my son, as they are too disturbing. He handed me the foil tube, and I tried to make it look like I was inhaling the smoke by sucking through the tube but not actually taking the smoke into my lungs, but he was wise to that. I even got a punch in my mouth for not doing it properly! I can still taste that first bitter taste of heroin in my mouth as I write this. I almost threw up after the first line. He fed me about four lines on a long sheet of foil. I've heard other users say that after the first taste of heroin, they were instantly hooked. From my experience, I can honestly say that yes, there is a good chance that one may be hooked after their first encounter. Maybe not everyone becomes instantly addicted but being instantly hooked and being instantly addicted are two different things in my eyes. Getting hooked simply means you return for the taste and the warm blanket feeling but being instantly addicted means your body feels it needs it rather than wants it. It's a very powerful drug, because after all Darren said and did to me in the flat that night, I forgave him and didn't blame him for a thing! How sick of me is that? He'd threatened to do physical damage to my boy, he'd done damage to me, and that dirty, stinking devil's dust washed away my parental instincts, emotions, and self-respect in a nanosecond. Oh well. What a brilliant way to start a relationship with the devil himself. Little did I know at the time that the abuse hadn't even started.

From that day onwards, taking heroin was not that scary to me. I suppose I experienced the fear of unknown before taking it, and now that I had, the fear had disappeared. I recall Darren giving me heroin 2-3 days a week to begin with and every time I took it, he would be in control of feeding it to me. I recall waking up one day and feeling like I had a cold. My nose was running, I was sniffling, sneezing, my eyes were teary and I felt uncomfortable. I thought to myself that it's only a cold, I'll get some medication later today when I go out to the chemist. Darren was in London and he happen to called me within a few minutes after me thinking of buying medication for my cold. Whilst on the phone to him, I mentioned that I have a cold. Darren laughed and said to me that I do not have a cold and that I am rattling. (A slang word for heroin detox). Darren told me to take 2 tablets that he had in a glass jar in the bedroom. The tablets were called DF118 and were a type of man made opiate. I took both tablets and within 5-10 minutes all of my cold symptoms had disappeared – completely! Darren also introduced me to crack cocaine. Crack cocaine opened my mind and I felt invincible. Within a few weeks, I became dependent on heroin and had a taste for crack cocaine. I was like a zombie.

After we'd been together for about six months, we ended up living in Southeast London in a one-bedroom flat, but my son stayed with my parents so he could continue to attend his school near to my mom's house. I also knew by then I was trapped, and it seemed no one could help me. Darren's idea was to set up home so that Josh could come and live with us. My idea was to wait until Darren was asleep one night and kill him and be totally free. Yes, even being in jail on a murder charge is freedom compared to being with someone you hate with a burning passion. I knew my son was never going to live with us in London, but I truly believed that one day soon I'd be free, and my boy and I could pretend that this nightmare had been just a bad dream. By now I was not only totally a slave to heroin but was also a lover of crack cocaine, and oh boy is that crack in a league of its own when it comes to addictions. I've seen it catch many people from all walks of life by the short and curlys. From solicitors to bank clerks, police officers, probation officers, common sex-workers, high-class sex-workers, prison officers, and average housewives. No one is above getting hooked on such powerful drugs. We committed crime to fund our enormous drug habit. Darren was always in control. He would place the tube in my mouth and tell me, "All you have to do is suck the smoke into the tube, and I'll do the rest." He even wanted to controlled my emotions—what little I had left. I had become numb. I'd gone from a healthy size 10 to a size 0 in a few weeks, my skin was grey and gaunt and in bad condition, my eyes were sunken, and my cheekbones stood out. He had complete control of my life. He told me to cut my hair quite short, and I felt that I had no choice but to obey him. It was easier that way. I even convinced myself that my hair suited me better now that it was short. I even lied to myself for fear of him. He chased me once to give me a beating because he said it was my fault that the local post office where we needed to go to cash a payment had closed. I tried to run for my life, but he eventually caught up with me, and I was so scared that I actually wet myself!

Another time I can recall is when I was getting ready to go out with him (we went everywhere together), and I was about to curl my hair. He demanded to do it, as I was his property. As he brought the hot curling tongs close to my forehead. I flinched. He got angry, saying he wouldn't burn me with the tongs and was angry because he wanted me to have trust in him. He brought the curling tongs close to my scalp a second time, and he did burn me that time. Admittedly it was a genuine accident, but he said that he hadn't touched my forehead and that I was exaggerating and that if there was not a burn on my forehead within 5-10 minutes and after the way I'd carried on, then I would pay for trying to make him feel guilty. I thanked God that a burn mark appeared on my forehead ten minutes later!

When I look back at the things I went through with this man, I know I'm truly blessed to be alive to tell this story. There were loads of times that man hit me and abused me, and you're probably asking yourself, "Why didn't she go back to her family?" "why did she stay with an abuser?" "Why did she not run for the hills the day she saw him do drugs?" I believe It's because pride and fear are one of the biggest and most powerful weapons in the emotional mind. I was full of pride as I did not want to admit that everyone was right about Darren. I also felt as though I had something to prove. I gave him a second chance the day I saw him take drugs on the day he was released as I genuinely believed he was telling the truth about him experiencing grief for the loss of his sister and that doing heroin that day was a one off. Most of the women I met in jail that were addicted to heroin had battle wounds, Darren looked really healthy and there were no evident signs of substance misuse and that is one of the reason's I believed him. The fear of being hurt by Darren if he ever caught me trying to get away, the fear of dealing with drug addiction alone and being too proud to return home to admit I failed. My pride couldn't take my parents seeing me like this. I was also very embarrassed. Some may ask, "Why didn't she go to the police?" When you live in the dark on drugs and crime, the police can be your number-one enemy. I also knew that if I went to the police about Darren, I would need evidence, I did not think I had any. No, I was too far gone in this dark drug lifestyle, and I believed that I would have to grin and bear it, as this was my life and I had to get on with it. I had never loved this man; in fact, I hated him with a burning passion so intense I could taste it. If you've ever been ruled by fear, then you know where I'm coming from. He used to give me pedicures and manicures, style my hair, and tell me what to wear and how to wear it, but these apparently nice acts were all done to increase my fear and his control. There was also a time before we moved to London when I had a bad pain in my back. I was standing in the kitchen complaining that my back was hurting. He said that I must take one of his antibiotics that his GP had given him. I told him that I could not take them, as I only had to say the word *antibiotic* and I got thrush. He insisted that I take a couple and that I'd be fine. He bullied me into taking this medication. It's the way he did it that still angers me to this day. He crushed the tablet and got a glass of fresh orange juice and put the powder into the juice. I protested and told him I would get thrush, but he ignored me, placed the orange juice on the kitchen side and just stared at me. I recall feeling very uncomfortable and so I picked up the glass of orange juice and drank it. The following morning, I woke up to discover that I had thrush! When I told him, he got mad at me and said that I was only telling him that to make him feel guilty! Mental torture is a terrible thing. He possessed me, and as I was weak and vulnerable, I allowed it to happen. I felt as if I were living in hell on earth and nobody could help me. Everywhere I went, he would be there tailgating me.

One day we were on our way back from his dad's flat, and we had a car parked in the car park near the flats. The car was not running, so he decided to tow it back to the flat we lived in. Darren was in a transit van and had the rope to tow the car back home. He told me to sit in the car, turn the key to unlock the steering wheel, and to leave a bit of slack to allow the van to pull the car without the rope snapping. Easy! It would have been if I had been living in a relaxed body, but whenever that man told me to do something, fear of getting it wrong gripped me with such a force that I physically shook and I would often get things wrong. In other words, I was a nervous wreck. He was my master, and I was his slave, and he spoke to me as if I were a child. He was a nasty piece of work. We set off, and I got it wrong a couple of times, but he didn't blow his lid. I gained a bit of confidence after we'd been driving for about twenty minutes and couldn't wait to get back to the flat, as I needed some heroin. He spotted one of his friends and pulled over to talk to him. We sat for a few minutes while he spoke to his friend, so I took the key out of the ignition and waited for him to finish talking. It all happened so quickly. He jumped back into the van, started up the engine, and began to take off. I panicked, as the key wouldn't turn in the ignition. The next thing I knew, the front wheel on the driver side of the car burst as it went over a Ballard and then the wheel at the rear of the car also on the driver side also burst. I was shouting out of the window to get Darren's attention, but he wasn't looking. He looked through his rear mirror as we approached a junction. When he saw what had happened, he flew out of the van and came to the car swearing and waving his arms about. I tried to explain what had happened, but it fell on deaf ears. He wasn't interested in what I had to say; he was angry, and I was getting the blame. He was absolutely demented! He began swearing at me and called me all the stupid cows under the sun. (I didn't know there were that many species of cows until that day). He began dragging me out of the car. Naturally, I tried to resist but failed miserably. Other motorists that were on the road nearby saw the commotion between me and Darren, and some men shouted abuse at him for ill-treating a woman. The traffic came to a halt, and there was a lot of angry motorists. The male motorists shouted at him to leave me alone and to pick on a man rather than a woman, but he didn't have anything to say to the men. He said to me that he believed that these men were lovers of mine, as they had no business getting involved with personal domestics. I wanted to tell the men in their cars to keep out of it, as it was making matters worse for me, although I know that if I'd done that, it would have made matters worse all around. He told me that this wasn't over and that when we get home, I'd get the beating of my life. I was petrified.

BOOK A DISCOVERY CALL WITH THE AUTHOR

Are you suffering with trauma? Have you been in an abusive relationship but feel you haven't been able to move on with your life? Do you feel as though you are still in a dark place and you are ready to come out? Book a discovery call with me by sending an email to at info@redflagwellbeing.co.uk

CHAPTER 5

THE DAY I TOOK CONTROL

We got home, and the abuse started as soon as we stepped into our "love nest." I then realised that this man was truly mad, sick in the head! When the abuse stopped, I looked at him coldly and said, "That is the last time you ever hit me again. Do you understand?" I must have said it with a chilling conviction that warranted his full attention, as I saw great fear in his eyes. It must have registered, as he didn't hit me again for a few weeks. That's when I tasted pure hate, because I understood that he *could* control his outbursts of anger. In that split second, my fear turned into hate, and I really don't know which of the two is worse! A few weeks after the incident and after my warning to him, Darren went to hit me. I picked up a hammer that was on the floor by the sofa and I hit him on the hip. After I tapped him on his hip, I put the hammer down on the floor and our eyes met. I said to him that I do not need a weapon and I recall placing my palms upwards as if to say bring it on! He was in shock and stood stock still, and I knew he had been given a dose of his own medicine. He wasn't very clever because he went to hit me again a few days later. The hammer had been removed from the living-room, and he obviously thought I'd got brave for just one day, so you can imagine his reaction when I jumped up and flew back at him. All fear of him left my body in an instant as I took his power from him. I had a tall, hollow ornament which I picked up and smashed it with force over his head. He cowered like a baby and shook with fear. The thing is, Darren had dreadlocks which were thick and covered his skull, the ornament was light and hollow, so why was he on the verge of tears? When I realised that he was a coward, I lost control and began to really go for him. I screamed at him, "Why are you crying baby? Surely this is nothing compared to what you've put me through!" I began smashing the flat to pieces, windows included. He sat in the armchair cowering and covering his head in his arms. I noticed that Darren was so frightened that he wet himself. Pathetic! I was in such a rage that I blacked out for a few minutes. I then realised that this joke called a relationship was in a very dangerous place. I now had control of the situation. He begged me to stop and said that if I wanted to go back to Birmingham, I had his permission. He really didn't get it, did he? If he thought for one second that I was about to walk away and leave him after what he'd done to me, he was stupider than I thought. No, this was payback time, and until I'd given him the torment and walking-on-egg-shells treatment he'd so easily given to me, I wasn't going anywhere. Anyway, who would keep me? I'd become completely dependent on him, as he held the golden key to my drug addiction. I spent the night at a mate's house and returned the next day for my daily fix, as my life depended on it. The fact that he had given me his permission to go back to Birmingham made me even more determined to stay just to prove to myself that I would no longer take any suggestion or command from this pathetic excuse for a man. I was no longer under lock and key. His telling me I was free to go was another way of saying, "I no longer have control over you," and I needed to stay around and prove that to him and to myself! It was very self-destructive, but I failed to see it that way, as the drugs had really blocked my perception of my reality.

I couldn't leave now, as I was totally trapped by the drugs, and the damage that man had done to my soul was not going to be mended for a long while, if at all. He had destroyed me with the drugs and the abuse I had endured on a regular basis. Did you know that when you're hooked on drugs its as if the devil has hold of your soul? The devil also has hold of your emotions when you're a slave to him through heroin. (I describe the devil as a negative dark force, not a man wearing a red cape). I wasn't going to walk out just like that. Not only had he taken total control of my life and made me totally dependent on him, but I really felt that I couldn't just go back to Birmingham in the state I was in. I was ashamed and believed I'd be judged and there would be lots of people in my family saying "I told you so." I decided that I wasn't going anywhere. All I wanted to do now was take back what was rightfully mine—my self-respect and dignity. Darren had got me on to hard drugs, and I needed him to keep on supporting me; after all, he had got me hooked. He could keep me but on my terms. I'd just become every man's worst nightmare! After all that happened that day, I believe the devil himself placed a ring on my finger for life, because something entered my mind. I went from frightened-for–her-life Kate to all-I-want-is-drugs-and-my-power-back Kate. On that night when I walked out to go spend the night at a mate's house, something massive changed in both of our lives.

The following morning, I had to return home to Darren, as he had the drugs and I needed some. After I'd had my fix, I just acted as if nothing had happened, but we both knew that something had taken place, and he was in a very dangerous position. As I only weighed about six stone, I thought I'd get myself sorted, start eating properly, and then go home to my parents and son—but not until I'd made his life complete hell for a while so that he'd have an idea what it was like to be on edge all the time! What I did not realise, was that non of this was true, I was lying to myself as I had become dependent on Darren and the drugs I lied to myself for months believing I was making the choices to stay in a destructive relationship. This was not really a conscious choice, it was now, co-dependency.

The only weight I added to my body came in the form of the ounces of heroin I picked up from our main supplier. At this point in our sad, sorry lives, we were making a lot of money through selling drugs. I became a secret crack smoker, as Darren had eased off smoking crack cocaine and mostly smoked heroin. So, I'd sneak out with about £150.00 per day to smoke crack cocaine in and around London. I smoked everywhere except at home unless it was really late at night; then I sneaked into the bathroom and locked myself in and smoked my drugs. There was even a time when I was so out of it that I got into the bath one night and woke up at around 9.30 a.m. the following morning! Whenever I look back and think of that time, I recognise that I am very fortunate and I can only describe this as God's Grace. We were making more than £1,000.00 a day selling heroin. I took charge to begin with, and when we got busy, I handed the reins over to him. I still sold drugs, but only on the rare occasions when a customer was considered dangerous. The reason I served this type of customer was that they trusted me, as they had only dealt with me when we first started selling. Darren also felt intimidated by anyone stronger than him!

One day I woke up from having a dream about police officers arresting Darren outside of the pub where we used to meet our customers who bought our wraps of heroin. The dream seemed so real that I was talking in my sleep, and Darren woke me up and asked what I was dreaming about. I told him about the dream and advised him that we should be more vigilant, as I believed that the dream was a sign. Later that day we got raided, but we were waiting for the police, as we acted on my vision. As you can imagine, police were a bit disappointed to say the least. The officers found no heroin but found some cannabis which Darren planted in the house to deter the drug dog from sniffing out our stash of heroin and it worked. Darren was charged with possession of a class B drug was taken to the police station where he received a caution and had to pay a £25.00 fine.

Another time when we were in the flat, there was a knock at the door. I went to the door and looked through the spy hole. I could see that it was one of Darren's cronies with another man that I had never seen before. As I was familiar with Darren's friend, I opened the front door. When I opened the door, I immediately saw a sawn-off shotgun. I screamed, and I'd be lying if I said I wasn't scared. Well, wouldn't you be with a sawn-off in your face? They made up some cock-and-bull story to rob Darren of his money and drugs. This is what happens when you are living the life of a drug dealer. I recall the fear of having to guard our home 24 hours a day as we never knew who our visitor would be. The biggest fear was being visited by someone who wants to rob you, or the police who want to do a drug bust. Most of the time I was out smoking drugs and buying drugs. A typical day could be described as waking up needing drugs, selling drugs all day and living in fear. Most of the time I would smoke the crack cocaine sitting on a staircase in a deserted block of flats or sat in my car and smoke for about 2 hours. I'd then either immediately go back to the dealer and score more crack or I would attempt to bring my anxiety down with heroin; about £20.00 worth would do it. I'd then score a lump of crack cocaine again but I'd buy say £100.00 worth, and go to a drug house, where I'd give the person who lived at the house a nice smoke of my drugs as that would secure me a seat in their home for the duration until my drugs ran out. It'd be late evening now, so I'd buy another £50.00 worth of crack cocaine to see me through the night. The beauty of selling heroin when you're an addict is that you don't have to go and score it, as it's there on tap. I often didn't know what time it was, and sometimes I didn't know what day it was either. Most nights I'd be up smoking crack cocaine and heroin until the early hours of the morning and that was why I was always up at the crack of dawn. Looking back at the situation I was in, I now understand where a lot of my unstable personality behaviour came from. As an addict, I recall not getting a good nights sleep so I suffered sleep deprivation and so sometimes I felt I was going out of my mind. I was out of my face twenty-four hours a day, seven. Days a week.

(Contact me at info@redflagwellbeing.co.uk if you or a loved one is suffering from trauma, mental health and or substance misuse, use the email link to book a discovery call to see if I can offer a solution to you.)

As time went by, there were about six other drug raids, but the police had bad timing; if they ever found anything, it was only a couple of wraps of heroin which Darren and I claimed as personal use. On the seventh raid, the police force's hard work and persistence paid off. On the day of the final drugs raid, Darren and I were both sat in our flat. We heard a loud bang on the front door. We both looked at each other with fear in our eyes. We sat there and heard the door banging. We heard a voice shout "police, open up!" Darren jumped up from his seat, grabbed a large parcel of heroin and threw it out of the window. Darren then followed the heroin and climbed out of the window and slid down the drainpipe. I was left in the flat on my own. I went and unbolted the front door to allow the police officers access to the flat. Some of the police officers entered the flat and some were outside where they found the parcel of heroin. They recovered most of the heroin which Darren threw out of the window but there was no sign of Darren. The police had to charge someone, and as I was the only person in the flat, that someone had to be me. The police knew that Darren had jumped out of the window, as he'd left it wide open. I didn't think to close the window, as I was in shock, and the neighbour below took pleasure in telling the police that he had seen Darren running down the road. The police also found a double-barrelled shotgun which Darren kept in the bedroom, which I said I didn't know anything about, and they believed me and said they'd be asking Darren about it when they caught up with him. The police knew that Darren had been in prison for possession of a firearm in the past. The fact that I was in the flat when the raid took place meant that I was also charged for possession with intent to supply. I was taken to the police station, where I gave a no-comment interview and was released the next morning. I found it strange that I was charged and then released but then I was released from the police station with a date to attend court in a few weeks. The police only gave me bail because they followed me knowing I would know where to find Darren and the police would have a lead to him. Of course, when I did see Darren, he realised why the police had bailed me, but he said he would hand himself in on Monday morning and take the charge. We only lasted a few days out together, as the person whose house we were staying at was being verbally abused by the way Darren spoke to him in his own home and he went to the police station where he informed the police of Darren's whereabouts. The police came crashing through the door early on a Monday morning and took Darren to the police station to question him about the drugs raid that had taken place in our flat. I was due to appear in court a few days after Darren's arrest However, due to my drug-fuelled lifestyle, I failed to appear at court. Consequently, I was on the run. A few weeks later I was arrested for shoplifting and remanded in police custody.

The next day, I was brought before Woolwich Magistrate Court the following day and the magistrates remanded me in custody to appear for sentencing in 4 months time. The CPS charged me with possession with intent to supply a controlled class A drug and failing to surrender to court after being granted bail from the police station. My solicitor made me aware that I was looking at quite a lengthy prison sentence for both offences.

There was a woman whom I met whilst on remand at HMP Holloway who informed me of another inmate who had an uncle who was in the Freemasons. I'd heard a couple of things about the Freemasons regarding the criminal justice system, however, I did not have any evidence that what I was told was true. I was led to believe that they were an organisation where special handshakes took place that allowed some criminals to get a lesser sentence or no sentence at all. Since 1997 whilst serving my first prison sentence, I'd practice contacting spirits through clairvoyance. This ability just came to me one day. I was able to clearly see people's past, present and future and I tapped into the spirit realm to hear from the spirits. I had a hunch to contact the spirits to tell me how to workout a code to do before the judge when I appeared in court. I really didn't fancy doing a few years in jail. The night before I was due in court for sentencing, I entered the spirit realm and contacted the demons who roam late at night (also known as ghosts); I was shown a sign and told how to do it. The spirit told me to do the sign there and then, so I did. Let me explain. That is what seeking the powers of darkness is all about. I was given a sign by my demonic agent. I pictured the sign in my mind but it felt as though I was transported to another spirit realm. It was strange as I felt as though I consciously left my body, travelled with my mind to the land of demons. This is the best way for me to articulate my experience. I performed the sign before the judge, who was known for being very harsh with sentencing, and he began to stutter after I made the sign, so I made it again, and he started to panic and stumble over his words. I couldn't believe what was happening right before my eyes. The judge said that this case should go to Crown Court, but he dealt with me in the Magistrates court by giving me a four-month custodial sentence! Was the sign I performed the sign that is used by a Freemason Member? Did the sign mean something specific to the judge that had nothing to do with the Freemason's? I don't know but what I do know is the sign I did got me a reduced prison sentence. I know that when a lot of people heard of my sentence, they immediately thought I was a police informer, as such a sentence is far too light for such a crime. At the time, I would rather have had people think that of me even though the truth is I invoked spirits to save my skin. People wouldn't have believed me, as the judge in question was well known for giving out harsh sentences for minor offences. I will talk about this more in another book concerning my true experiences of walking with dark power. I was given a four-month custodial sentence, and as I'd spent a few weeks in custody already, I didn't have very much left to do. My release date was set for mid-December that year.

CHAPTER 6

RETURNING HOME TO BIRMINGHAM

Eventually I was released from prison and went to stay at a mate's house in Catford, London. She was also a drug addict, and consequently we sat and smoked heroin and crack cocaine until the early hours of the morning. Although I came out of prison drug free as I had done my heroin detox within the first 3-4 weeks of being in jail, so by now, I had no withdrawal symptoms, but mentally I was still very much addicted. A lot of people who are not addicts may not understand the intense power of certain drugs and the strong hold they can have over your mind and ultimately your life.

Thankfully my older brother managed to contact me, and we arranged for me to go back home to my family in Birmingham, who were very worried about my well-being. I wanted to be home for Christmas.

I returned to my mom and dads on Christmas Eve 2000. It was very emotional seeing my long-lost family after what seemed a lifetime. It was too painful to put into words, especially when I saw my baby after being apart for so long.

It didn't take long before I was caught up in the rat race and was using drugs even more than I had when I lived in London. I cashed one of my younger brother's GIRO payments with the intention of replacing the money as soon as I had sorted myself out as I was suffering with withdrawal symptoms, but he was informed by the post office when he enquired about his missing GIRO. The guilt I felt was unbearable, but because I did a couple of things that people do when they're sold out to heroin and crack, I felt as if I had murdered someone. That was often the way I felt whilst taking those drugs. Truth be told, I probably would have found it easier to live with murder than the hurt I put my family through. Before I knew it, I was shoplifting giant legs of lamb, joints of beef, and so on. I soon moved on to bigger things, such as clothing from fashion shops. I'd been caught shoplifting a few times and had been given fines and community rehabilitation orders, but none of them seem to work for me at that time. I got sent to HMP Brockhill, Redditch. I was there from November 2001 and was in a cell next door to a woman whom I'd met in prison back in 1997 when I was in for the post office theft. We got on well. My mate had converted to the Islamic religion and told me things about her religion. She encouraged me to give up crime and the lifestyle that came with it and become a Muslim. However, when heroin came into the jail, she was one of the first ones to obtain it and so we both took it and we both smoked it on tin foil.

My mate showed me how to pray correctly to Allah and explained how to do the *Wu ju* (the wash before you can pray). She also told me how many times a day one is expected to pray and showed me the prayers that one must pray to worship. I read through the prayers and wanted to find out more about this religion, as it sounded very easy. She told me that the Qua-ran was written in the same language all over the world and said that the Bible contradicts itself and has many translations; that, she said, was one of the reasons people don't understand it. Because I was very confused by the Bible growing up and didn't really understanding the distinctions between God, Jesus, the Lord, and the Holy Spirit, when she told me that Muslims pray directly to Allah, who is their God, it all seemed much easier to me. In the past, I had stayed away from all this religion stuff because it seemed too confusing. I was learning the main Islamic prayer in English, but then my mate told me that the prayer was void unless it was spoken in Arabic. As I was so determined to say this prayer, I asked her to speak the prayer in Arabic, and I wrote it out as it was pronounced on a piece of paper. For two days I sat in my cell and practised the prayer in Arabic, and after those forty-eight hours I had learned the main prayer so that I could pray correctly to Allah. I was sceptical, because there's no way you can put your heart into something you don't feel in your heart, and I found it impossible to express what I wanted to talk to God about but my mate told me that you can only pray that way to draw closer to Allah. I was told that the good thing about this prayer was that anything you asked for would be done. I also understood that prayer is not just for asking God for something. Although my life had spiralled out of control, I still felt that I had a lot to thank God for too. But how could I ask for anything or express true gratitude that I truly desired to do if I wasn't allowed to do it from my heart in the language that I have spoken all my life? So, this religious thing was confusing me again and I was told that if I prayed in my native language, I would not be heard or accepted! So, let me get this right—if you don't pray in Arabic, then your prayer is void? By now I'd gone from confused to confused.com! Something inside of me knew that there was a God and that He accepts our prayers no matter what language we speak in. When I had found myself in trouble or a vulnerable situation, I had certainly felt a great power guiding me I also did my best to ask God for help when I was in a tricky situation and somehow, I was led out of those situations and I did not pray in Arabic. I will say that the discipline in the Islamic religion is intense, as you must pray 7 times a day and at certain times every day. Now let's move on.

I was released from HMP Brockhill on 7 March 2002. The next day I went to the local hospital to visit my nan (my mom's mom), as she had been diagnosed with cancer and admitted into hospital on the day of my prison release. The family had been told that nan only had a few days left, and we were very upset, to say the least. Nan stayed with us for a lot longer than the doctor predicted. On 17th April 2002, Nan took her last breath. We were all devastated at the loss. I was with her as she took her last, precious breath. I found it quite painful, but I also felt relief, as Nan was a staunch Christian, and although I didn't believe in Jesus Christ, I believed that she had gone to a better place. Just when I thought nothing could get worse, my Granny died nine weeks later, also of cancer. Losing both grandmothers in a matter of nine weeks to cancer was devastating for us all.

When I first came out of prison, I managed to stay focused and didn't really do drugs. I dabbled (dabbling means doing drugs on a part-time basis), but after the death of both my grandmothers, I went off the rails, as I found the pressure of living with reality too much to bear. Losing one nan was traumatising. When my mommy (my grandma who I called mommy) also went, I thought I was going to lose my mind. No one had any idea of the damage that did to me. I woke up with pain in my heart first thing in the morning and real tears filled my eyes. Then I'd remember something about her just by looking at my dad, as he resembled her so much, and I'd fill up with tears all over again. I wept myself to sleep some nights. I would hear her voice in my head. My mind was very noisy with intrusive thoughts to harm myself and the best way for me to block them out was to turn to the drugs.

On the day of Mommy's funeral, I stood over her open coffin, and my tears ran down my cheeks uncontrollably. I wet her lifeless body with the tears of true love. One of my aunts had to prise me away from the coffin so that the undertaker could replace the lid to her coffin so that she could be taken to her final resting place. Not long after Mommy's funeral, my drug habit escalated to another level—a level that I had to maintain, as withdrawing is painful. When you withdraw from drugs not only do your emotions hit you hard, but your body is screaming in pain until you get that next fix. The mind is in constant negativity and the world is seen as a very dark place. I still prayed to Allah, so in effect I was practising Islam for a few months after my release in March of that year.

After the funerals of both my grandmothers, I recall sitting in my room and doing drugs. I suddenly had an idea and I whispered to myself "I wonder what it would be like to be drug free?" I then found myself imagining a life with no drugs. I felt so peaceful and happy, and I was outside of time, it felt amazing! When I opened my eyes and saw my current reality, I would feel sad but, I now had a secret place to escape hell.... It was my imagination. Over the next few years, I used my imagination to escape the drugs world. I actually imagined myself living the life I am currently living now. Every time I visited my imagination, my vision got bigger, clearer and clearer. I did not resist my current situation, nor did I realise that I had unlocked a very powerful faculty of our marvellous mind, but I did it and it was effortless.

(Do you know how powerful the imagination faculty is? Book a discovery call to work with me on HOW to use the imagination to create from a place of ease at info@redflagwellbeing.co.uk

From 2002 to 2011, I was in and out of prison more times than I care to remember; I would like to share some of the things I witnessed and experienced whilst I toured some of the female prisons in the UK.

Almost every time I got arrested and sent to jail, I either had a parcel of heroin with me or I met another inmate with a parcel of gear on her. Does the saying "the devil looks after his own" spring to mind? I recall being sent to HMP Brockhill, and because I was on the run, I always had my gear with me. I was sent to jail and had something like eleven wraps of heroin on me. I made it my business to find out who was already locked up so I could have a little wrap for them when I had my welcome party. I arrived at the prison when all the other girls were banged up for the night, which meant I had to become a window warrior for the night. I got talking to a girl who was on the same wing as me, but she was upstairs on the second level. When I realised that we were from the same area and we knew each other, she made a swing using a tea-pack bag (one of the brown paper bags that the prison canteen put our daily teabags, sugar, and whiteners in) and a dressing-gown belt and lowered the bag down to me. I popped a jail wrap in the bag, and she pulled it up to her window, and Bob's your uncle she now has some heroin!

I recall going to HMP Eastwood Park a few times too. There was always someone on the induction wing with a parcel of heroin. If it wasn't me, then another girl would have a parcel in their possession. The prison guards were wise to the goings-on on the wing but were limited as to what they could do. Some guards would leave you to take your drugs and then the next day, you would be frog marched to the prison block or reception unit to do a urine test. As drugs stay in the body for a few days, we weren't drug tested when we were first brought in, which gave us time to have a smoke and not get added grief. The number of drugs I witnessed in that jail alone was phenomenal.

The time I spent in jail wasn't always focused on drugs. Some of the things that happened behind prison walls were funny! I will always recall the times when we were allowed to have karaoke. I was an MC, and my MC name was Gangsta that also became my nickname in the prison. I wasn't shy about grabbing the mike and being the centre of attention. There were lots of talented women in prison with voices that would put a lot of pop stars to shame. I found that there was always someone who was creative and good at art. Looking back at some of the women that I did time with a lot of them were lost souls caught up in the rat race because of the cares of the world, and it was a real eye-opener. I was also a lost soul just going through the motions. It was a sad and lonely place.

I met a lot of girls whilst I toured. There's a funny tale to tell from almost every prison sentence I did. There was a time when I was almost unconscious on heroin, and I had the bright idea to sue the prison service. I had smoked heroin during the night and was absolutely intoxicated to the point I could not keep my eyes open. When I woke up the next day, I was still very drowsy as the drugs were quite potent. I wanted to get out of my cell for one reason or another, so I filled a jug from the tap and tipped the water onto the floor, got my mate to press the cell bell, and lay on the floor groaning and holding my left side. The officer who came to our cell was what was known as an old-school screw, meaning he had been an officer for many years and knew every trick in the book. As soon as the officer saw me, he rolled his eyes to the ceiling at my performance and said, "Up you get, Spencer. The act's over." I pretended to be dazzled as if I had been knocked unconscious, but he decided to allow me to have my moment and waited patiently. My speech was slurred, because I really was high on the drugs from the night before. My mate helped me up, but she was having trouble keeping her face serious. Then I began limping on my left leg, but I had my hand on the right side of my back. The officer looked at me, and he couldn't help but laugh, saying, "How did you end up on the floor?" I said that I'd slipped and landed on my left side and banged my head and I wanted a doctor. I looked a complete idiot, as I was limping on the wrong foot, my T-shirt was wet on the right side, and the puddle of water on the floor was in the wrong place to match my story! I got to see the doctor and got some strong painkillers, but the officer laughed at my attempt to lodge an official complaint to get any sort of compensation!

I was also known for making toast in my cell with a taper (tissue paper made into a wick and then set alight with a lighter or matches). I would stand and cook toast in my cell, filling the prison wing with the smell of fresh toast. A few officers tried to catch me in the act cooking the toast but were always too late, apart from one officer who nobody really liked—there was always one. I was making toast in my cell, and this officer walked in and caught me buttering my freshly cooked toast. Rather than leave me alone with my breakfast, he decided to tackle me. He went to grab my toast, and I quickly moved my hand. We played the cat-and-mouse game of him trying to get my toast and me not giving it over. In the end, he gave me a verbal warning for making toast in my cell, but I had the last laugh: I kept my toast and ate it!

When I tell you that there are people from all walks of life behind bars, I'm not kidding you. One of the most disturbing sentences I did was in 2000 in Holloway. There was a woman who was on remand for the murder of her daughter. She denied killing her child and was always very timid when walking around the prison until one day another inmate pushed in front of her whilst we queued for our dinner. She turned on the queue jumper nastily, and everyone who witnessed it was shocked. She also walked around telling anyone who'd listen to her about her baby, who had dropped dead outside of a church. Someone told me that she was innocent, and I had to ask her myself. The woman had lots of documents that she said were from professional doctors who stated that the little girl had no suspicious circumstances surrounding her death. Her story set off alarm bells in my head, but if you saw how humble, shy, and extremely good natured she appeared to be, you too would have been led to believe that she was another innocent woman locked away for a crime she didn't commit. Her story was that she had been in church and her daughter had been misbehaving, so she said that she had smacked her, and because her daughter had dropped to the floor and died outside of the church that day, other church members had reported her to the police and said that she'd hit the child, causing her death. That's what set the alarm bells off in my head. I never hit my son, but I am pretty sure that if I ever did, he would not have died from it! She had photos of her and her daughter, and yes, they looked very happy together. She always walked around the prison with her Bible gripped tightly under her arm, and sometimes she had photos of the little girl who had died placed in her Bible.

I had been to court one day and was sent back to prison on remand and was in reception having a meal and waiting to be taken back to my cell when this woman sat opposite me. She had some photos on the dining table and was admiring them and telling me that she missed her baby. It was quite emotional for me. I don't recall the reason, but at one point some of us were to lodge overnight in different cells on different wings, and I was put in a four-bed cell with this woman and two others. I knew one of the women, as I had shared a cell with her when I first came to HMP Holloway in September of that year, so we were having a natter and a laugh about prison life. The next thing I knew, this lady who was on a murder charge was standing by the cell door speaking to an officer. I couldn't hear what she was saying, as she spoke softly. However, I clearly heard the officer reply something like, "You'll have to go one night without it; I'm not going to bring you another one!" I was gobsmacked when I heard the way this officer spoke to the woman, because this particular officer was very fair and very professional and often had a kind word for us girls. I then found out that the woman had left her Bible in reception and was requesting a Bible for the night. So why was this officer so rude to her? I did not know why but I recall sleeping peacefully that night.

A few days later when I was back on my allocated wing, I was chilling on my bed. An officer came into my cell and took our little portable radio which was on a table and removed all of the newspapers. I wondered what was going on at first, but I found out later that all the radios and newspapers around the prison were confiscated that day, so obviously there was something happening in the outside world that they didn't want us prisoners to hear about.

I was attending Woolwich Magistrates court a few days later when I realised that something was very wrong. There were about seventy women in the changing area all wearing bright blue prison dressing gowns and flip-flops and waiting to be searched before we were led out of the prison and placed into the prison van (Also known as a sweat-box) that was taking us to court. After what seemed an age, I was seated on the sweat box. I sat in front of a girl who I knew from the prison. We were talking in what's known as back slang. I had smuggled a lighter past the officers, and she wanted a light for her roll-up. I put it under my door and was just about to slide the lighter to her when a black boot gently trod on my fingers. When I looked up to see an officer smiling down at me, I told her to get her boot off my hand. She removed her foot but was still standing outside my door. The girl behind me started shouting to a woman who was sitting quietly at the rear of the bus. She was situated so that there wasn't a prisoner in the cubicle opposite hers. The girl behind asked the silent woman in the rear cubicle various questions, such as, "When did you come on the bus, love? How come you're in the corner hidden away from the rest of us? What's the big secret?" The woman wouldn't answer the questions. I then discovered that it was the woman who was on remand for the murder of her daughter. She had been put on the bus first while the rest of us were waiting in our dressing-gowns to be searched. I said to the girl behind me, "She's accused of killing her daughter, but she didn't do it." I was convinced that she hadn't murdered her daughter, because I had been told by a fellow inmate that she had documentation from an outside doctor stating that her daughter had collapsed and died from an illness that had gone undetected while the child was alive. I also saw some documents but I did not read them in detail but in my opinion they looked like legal legitimate documents. I called out to the woman and asked her if she was all right. She didn't answer me. The officer appeared in front of me and asked me why I was asking the woman if she was all right. I said, "Because she's innocent. She didn't do it." The officer slid a newspaper under my door and said, "How can you call what she done innocent?" I read the article in the paper regarding the woman's charge, but it didn't say anything I didn't know. The reporter had made her sound guilty already!

That was the day I received my four-month custodial sentence, and I'd done a few weeks on remand, so I didn't have long left to serve. I got transferred to HMP Highpoint a few days after being sentenced. Numerous prisoners told me that a well-known convicted child murderer who'd committed a string of offences with her partner back in the 1970s was down the block at HMP Highpoint but I didn't see her. I'm sharing this bit of information with you to show that I was in jail with people from all walks of life.

When I was back in Birmingham after Christmas in 2000, I sat watching the news with tears streaming down my face. They were tears of anger and deep sorrow mixed. There on my mom's wide-screen TV was a photograph of the little girl that I had seen whilst I was in HMP Holloway a few weeks before. The nice lady with the Bible was described as an evil aunt who had murdered her niece who had been sent to England from France to have a better life. This woman had been successful at fooling social services, and the news pointed this information out as a fact. If I hadn't met the woman myself, I'd probably have shared the majority opinion of the country, which held that social services had failed this child and had chosen to ignore the warning signs. This woman was a very calm and placid person. I've always had a sixth sense, and even though I had my suspicions about the way the supposedly nice woman told her story about how her daughter had dropped dead outside of her local church, and even though I had seen a nasty side to her that day when the other inmate had pushed in front of her, and even though I had seen the officers treat her like trash, and despite the fact she didn't acknowledge me when I called out to her on the sweat box, her body language told a totally different story. I can see how she fooled social services. I must stress that this woman had the whole jail fooled, and most of the women there were hardened criminals who did not miss a trick. This woman was found guilty of murder. Sometimes in prison you don't know who your next-door neighbour is.

All sorts of things ran through my mind after watching the news. I was angry, because when I replayed the encounters, I had had with this woman and saw how she was, I was disturbed. Of course, there was nothing I could have done that would have brought that little girl back into the world, but I did wonder what I would have done if I'd known the full story when I had to sleep in a bed next to that woman. I think a lot of women would be asking themselves the very same question.

Overall, I found that prison can either make you or break you. It made me stronger in the sense that I got hardened to prison life, and sometimes I looked forward to being sent to jail for a break and a bit of rehab. It was the one time my family could be certain that I was not on the street or dead in a gutter. My mom told me once that my dad was tormented by the thought that the police would knock the door one night and ask him to come and identify my dead body. So, I can confirm that my family slept easier at night when I was behind bars, as they knew where I was morning, noon, and night. I've always looked at jail as easy, but I have come to realise it's easier for the hardened criminal; I was in and out of jail for years and became comfortable with it. However, I was very selfish in that respect, because I have it on good authority that it wasn't easy for my family. Because my drug habit was a big one, I welcomed jail, and I still believe that going to jail as often as I did saved my life, because many times I was knocking on death's door.

I also remember a story that always makes me giggle when I recall it. I was not in prison on this occasion but I was sat in my mums house one day. One of my younger sister's had arrived at my mum's with her friend. My sister called Joanne and her friend Julie, were talking about going to Handsworth to buy some West Indian takeaway food. I recall my mouth watering as I imagined curried goat, ox-tail, fried dumplings and rice and peas. I asked Joanne and Julie if I could please go with them to get some food. They both said yes. Julie was driving, Joanne sat in the passenger seat and I sat in the back on our way to get the food. When we arrived at the take-away, I offered to go in to the shop to order and wait for our food. I collected the money from the ladies and went into the shop. After about 15 minutes, I came out of the Caribbean take away holding a carrier bag which contained our delicious food. I skipped to the car and as I was so happy to be eating one of my favourite dishes I began singing an uplifting song. I opened the car door, jumped in the back and continued singing at the top of my voice. I opened the carrier bag and began to take out my meal. I looked up to give the ladies their meal when I saw 2 men looking at me from the driver and front passenger seat. I stopped singing and realised I had jumped in the wrong car. The 2 men didn't say a word, they just starred at me. I quickly apologised as I got out of the car. I then noticed Joanne and Julie sat in the car behind. They were laughing so hard they couldn't even talk. When they managed to stop laughing, they said that they had tried to get my attention when they saw me open the door of the car in front but they said they couldn't alert me from them both being doubled over with laughter.

The last time I was sentenced and sent to prison was on 28 October 2010. The weird thing is that I had a strange feeling that this was my last time in shackles. I was only doing a six-month sentence, so it was a short stay. I started my sentence in HMP Foston hall in Derbyshire. After I'd been there for a few weeks, I was transferred to HMP Drakehall. When I only had 3 weeks left of my sentence, I had an appointment to go to the resettlement building in the prison. I was asked if I had suitable accommodation to return to upon discharge. Prior to going in to prison I was classed as homeless as I did a lot of sofa surfing from one drugs den to another. The resettlement team asked me if I had a specific area that I would like to live in. I opened my mouth and blurted out an area that is about 6 miles from the city centre, but it was an area that I did not desire. I had no idea why I said that and I was not familiar with that area except from when I went to the High Street to shoplift. As soon as the words were out of my mouth, the resettlement officer smiled and said that there is a vacancy in a supported accommodation in that area. I was asked some questions while the officer completed a referral form and then I saw a housing officer who said they would see me next week with a decision of accommodation. In less than 7 days, I was called to the resettlement building and told that I was accepted in a supported accommodation called Pauline's Supported Accommodation.

Whilst in Drakehall, I met some really good girls on that sentence. Most of the women I spoke to were in prison for a silly mistake and it was their first time in jail. There was a Nigerian woman who lived on the same house block as me who everyone called Mommy, as she was the mothering type. She was an inspiration to us all. Mommy use to bring us food from the kitchens and we felt her peaceful presence whenever she was around. She had something about her that we all trusted and loved. She was a very spiritual woman who prayed for me when I was at the prison gates the morning that I was being released from HMP Drakehall. She held on to me and prayed in tongues a bear whisper and would not let me go. She had tears in her eyes, and I knew that whatever she prayed for me was deep. My memory jolted, I have heard this language before! This was the language I heard and spoke in my dream when I was on a beach with an immaculate being! The ladies who stood to say their goodbyes looked sad. We had some great memories of that prison sentence. I can tell you that the girls who were in Exeter House over Christmas and New Year will have a few stories to tell their grandchildren in years to come. Let's just say that we welcomed 2011 in with a bang! We didn't get back to the house until 3 a.m. New Year's Day! We also had parties, watched DVDs on the weekend, and were there for each other. It wasn't just some of the girls who were in Exeter House that I hung out with. There were a few girls spread out over the jail that I became good mates with too. We had a special bond, and the night before I went home, we had an invitation-only leaving party. I was a first-class comic; no wonder I was called Prankster and not Gangsta sometimes! I'd studied a handful of characters within the jail and decided to put on a show by mimicking their traits. I know that night is still talked about today, as it was a leaving party none of the girls will ever forget! I dressed up, wore wigs, used gold coloured paper to make a gold tooth, the laughter was so good for the soul. The girls laughed until they had tears running down their cheeks.

I slept like a baby the night before I was released. After I'd said all my good-byes and done a lot of crying, I was released from HMP Drakehall on 27th January 2011. Eventually I was on the train on my way to Birmingham. I had a very strange feeling. I knew something was going to happen, but I couldn't put my finger on it. Whilst in prison I had been on a methadone script, and I had done a detox programme to come off the methadone, which meant that for the last three to four weeks of my sentence, I was completely drug free. However, I felt ill, as I was still withdrawing. It's a slow and painful process, so basically, I still felt like crap. Prior to my release date, I would entertain the drug filled ideas that swam around in my head. In my opinion, the worst part of drug addiction is the war within. I didn't have a strong urge to go and get drugs immediately after release, and that was very strange, but, I still had drug related thoughts swimming around in my head. Before this prison sentence, I met a man called Doug. Doug was a bit of a loner and he owned a car. We met in a drug house and we got talking. When he heard that I was a shoplifter, he offered to be my driver. Doug's personal hygiene was very poor but I wasn't going into a relationship with him, he was only going to be my driver so I didn't let it concern me. I would go out for around 2 hours and I would pay Doug £100.00 a day as I could steal up to £600-700 worth of clothing some days and so I did not miss £100.00. I contacted Doug and asked him to meet me in Stechford. As soon as I met up with my mate Doug, who was also a drug addict, I wanted to get off my face and take as many drugs as possible as I was not willing to live the life of a heroin addict any more. I scored some crack and heroin, and we went to his flat and smoked all afternoon and all night. I was supposed to go to a supported accommodation to reside, as I was homeless upon release, but Doug said I could stay over at his on the sofa and if I still wanted to go to the hostel the following day he'd drop me over, as he knew the area well. I recall buying a 1 litre bottle of Irish cream whiskey which I also drank that night. I wanted to overdose and end my life so I drank the 1 litre bottle mixed with class A drugs and drifted off to sleep.

The following morning, I woke up and felt very rough. I had smoked a lot of drugs, and I'd drunk the bottle of Irish cream. It's a wonder I woke up at all. When I woke up that morning, I felt exactly like I had felt in the past after taking drugs but I felt a bit worse. I heard another person's voice in Doug's flat. I went to the bathroom, and when I came out, I saw a man sitting with my mate smoking heroin. He offered me some, but I said no thanks. I wanted to kick myself for refusing, but there was definitely something in me that wanted to get away from the drugs at that particular time. I had no idea what it was; I just knew that it wasn't my strength or my will. The reason I can affirm that it was not my strength is that I wanted to say yes but the word no came out instead. I also felt an external force turn me away from Doug's friend, it was like I was being guided.

CHAPTER 7

THE POWER OF TRANSFORMATION

When I was ready to leave Doug's flat with Doug, we made our way over to Pauline's supported accommodation. Doug entered the property with me as he was helping to carry some of my belongings. As soon as I walked in the door, I felt safe and the place was peaceful, but I could not explain it in words. The lady who owned the premises came out of her office to meet and greet me. The lady also greeted Doug. I instantly felt power coming from this woman, but it was not the power I recognised. The spirit that was in me tried to reject her, and I recall saying to her, "I can see through people," warning her that I was Gangsta. She looked straight back at me and said, "I too can see through people," and I knew she wasn't lying. I did not like her, but I was drawn to her, and it threw me off guard. She didn't rise to me, and she didn't back down either. I didn't know what was happening, but I knew it was a force stronger than my own. I was used to people having respect for me or totally disliking me. I've heard people say, "Like her or hate her; either way you have to rate her," referring to me and my drug lifestyle. A resident who introduced herself as Elaine showed me around the supported accommodation and then showed me to room 1, which was where my bed awaited. As soon as I stepped foot in that room, I knew that I wouldn't be doing drugs there, but not because of the smoke alarm or anything physical. It was intuitive, but I didn't know what it was at the time. It was a strange feeling I felt in that house, but I couldn't quite understand what was going on.

Earlier on, I had planned to go shoplifting with my mate Doug, but I wanted to go out alone. Doug would be my driver whilst I went into the shops to steal. It was a selfish desire, but I didn't need him with me—it was extra money I'd have to pay out, and I was quite sick of supporting men with drug habits. However, we went out as planned, but after I'd sold my stuff, I didn't have the strong urge to score drugs. When I was around Doug, for some unknown reason, I suddenly realised that I didn't like it, because he reminded me of heroin and crack. He hadn't done anything wrong; in fact, he said that he didn't want drugs that day too, so he dropped me off at the supported accommodation, and I cooked myself a meal and stayed indoors. I used tinfoil to aid me when I shoplifted, and the sight of the foil would trigger me to think of heroin and crack cocaine, but that day it had no mental effect on me. In all the years that I smoked heroin; the sight of foil had automatically triggered my brain to think about the drugs. That day, the thought didn't come into my mind. Looking back now, I thought it was strange, and I didn't dwell on it too much. That night, before I drifted off to sleep, I recall having a feeling of dread as I knew I would be detoxing in the morning. The following day I woke up and decided to have a shower before making a cup of tea. I grabbed my towel and toiletries and headed for the communal shower room. After my shower, I got dressed and made myself a hot drink. Although I had not spoken with Doug today, I had a gut feeling that he would arrive at the supported accommodation to take me out shoplifting. I decided to wear my housecoat over my clothes as I had a feeling that Doug would arrive unannounced and if he did, then I would say I was not dressed. Doug came around to pick me up, but I was on the sofa in the residential lounge with my quilt draped over me, and I told him that I didn't want to go out grafting that day and I lied saying I was unwell. After he'd gone with a bee in his bonnet, I got ready and went out shoplifting alone. He really reminded me of something negative but I did not know what it was and I couldn't stand being around him for that reason. Something was happening to me, and I had no control over this change whatsoever as I had not realised this at all. The next day I did the same: I went shoplifting, sold my things, made my money, and came back to the supported accommodation and chilled out for the night. The following day I got up early, got dressed, and went to the phone box to call him to let him know I wasn't going out grafting again, but I could tell by his voice that he wasn't happy. When I was out shoplifting, the sight of the tinfoil and the drug dealers' mobile numbers stored in my phone had absolutely no effect on me whatsoever but I was totally oblivious to this at the time. I went out on my travels, made my money, and returned to the supported accommodation. When I returned that night, Elaine, another resident, told me that my mate Doug had turned up whilst I was out, let himself onto the property, and had been just about to walk straight into my room when the service manager who was named Pauline saw him and told him to get off her premises. When I heard that, I knew that he wouldn't be back, and I gave the service manager a high 5 in my mind.

I felt that there was something about the service manager who I will refer to as Pauline We didn't hit it off when we first met, but I had a grudging respect for her. I couldn't put my finger on what it was about this lady. I knew she was a Christian, and I could feel positivity coming off her in big waves, but we didn't connect spiritually. When I had been in the supported accommodation for roughly 2 days, she took me aside and sat me down. I though she was doing the formalities with paperwork but she stood in front of a whiteboard and began drawing a stick-person. She wrote down our 6 higher faculties and she began to explain the science of thinking. I did not understand but I understood if that makes any sense. It was a weird experience as what this lady was showing me seemed to resonate with my soul but my conscious mind could not grasp its depth. One of our first real conversations was about the church that she attended, and my immediate response was to tell her that I didn't do church. She just smiled at me and said OK. The other residents had told me that you had to attend church or else you'd be asked to leave! I was shocked, and I waited for the woman to tell me this as well. Not everyone who lived in the supported accommodation attended church, so that turned out not to be true. I also never heard her say that to anyone, so I saw it as idle gossip but I did sense that some of the residents acted different in her presence and all of them spoke behind her back but where nice to her face. I decided to keep my distance from everyone as I was not there to make any friends and their attitude was not very good so I distanced myself by going out every day. On one occasion, Pauline did mention that I should come to her church but I do not like being bothered by people who seem to force their beliefs on others and she did mention God to me once, and my immediate response was, "I'm a Muslim." I wasn't, but it was the only religion I'd practiced, so I used it to distract her.

After I'd been in the supported accommodation for about a week, I settled into a routine of waking up at 7 a.m., showering, dressing, and going out on my shoplifting mission. One day I woke up with the intention to go out as normal, but my body wouldn't let me. I felt lethargic and lifeless. I got my quilt and snuggled up on the sofa in the lounge. My body felt heavy, peaceful and relaxed but I felt strange. I wasn't ill or anything; it was as if I had a heavy burden on me, but I didn't know why. This happened to me for three days. I just lay on the sofa with no get-up-and-go. The service manager Pauline saw me lying on the sofa but never said a word to me. I had often seen her shout at the other residents for being in the communal area wearing their nightwear but she never uttered a word to me when she saw me lying on the sofa with my quilt wearing pyjama's. After the three-day lie-down, I was up and running again. I still didn't have the urge or desire to do drugs, and I do not recall any thoughts on being a drug addict. I began to feel different and very strange. It was as if a huge burden had been lifted off my shoulders.

I also recall one day when I bumped into Pauline as she was coming out of her office. We both said our hellos, and then she said to me, "God said He wants you to come to church." I said, "I don't do church, and could you please not ask me again, as I definitely will not be going!" After my confusion about God growing up learning a little bit about the Islamic faith back in 2001–2002, church was the last place I wanted to go. Don't get me wrong—I went to weddings, funerals, and christenings, but those were the only times I actually stepped foot in a church. I knew that God existed, as I'd never believed in evolution but something from within told me that God was not who most people say He is.

Although I wasn't taking drugs any more, I started to have a drink with some of the residents in the house when Pauline. went home. At first it was the odd drink here and there to socialize, but then it became a regular thing in my life. I would drink to get drunk. My addictive personality was still at large. This frightened me, as I recalled Pauline and a resident named Clarke talking about a Bible passage (Luke 11:24–26). In this passage, Jesus says, "When an unclean spirit goes out of a man, he goes through dry places, seeking rest; and finding none, he says, 'I will return to my house from which I came.' And when he comes, he finds it swept and put in order. Then he goes and takes with him seven other spirits more wicked than himself, and they enter and dwell there; and the last state of that man is worse than the first.'" I recall thinking, "Oh my God! I'm clean from heroin and crack cocaine, and now the drink wants to take over and attack me seven times as much; I had better take this drinking easy!" (**For a deeper understanding of this paragraph, book a discovery call by contacting me at <u>info@redflagwellbeing.co.uk</u>**)

As time went on, I still went out almost every day to shoplift and make money from it to buy the nice things in life. Most things I shoplifted, but things like my Ugg boots and my Ugg scarf I paid for with cash. I also went and paid for some Adidas Cribs. Those are just a few of the many things I acquired through my grafting. My collection of belongings was getting to a point where I wouldn't need to buy or steal for a very long time. My wardrobe was growing at such a rate that I seriously considered investing in a new wardrobe. I had high-end toiletries, fashion jewellery, perfumes, nightwear, and even optical wear (I paid extra, as I received an NHS voucher because I was claiming benefits). I paid extra for my glasses; I chose a pair of designer frames and had the lenses thinned out. I also invested in disposable contact lenses, which I paid for with cash. In the space of one month, I'd easily made a few thousand pounds including the clothes and all the other things I now owned, and I always had money in my pocket. I recall waking up one morning about a week after coming out of jail and doing my make-up and hair in the mirror. I had to look not once or even twice but three times, because I no longer resembled the old me! I woke up, and over twenty years had left me! Not just my face but my hair also looked different. My hair was full of life, bouncy, and in good condition. The skin on my face and my body was youthful, and my figure was taking on a new shape. I was using the same soap and body lotion I'd used all my life, so what was going on? I also had a prolapsed womb and was due to go to see my doctor to make an appointment to see a gynaecologist, but that had also disappeared! What was going on? I walked down the road and people stared at me. They were not the stares I'd become used to when I was on drugs; no, these were looks saying,

"Who's this woman?" I got lustful stares from men of all ages; women looked at me with admiration, envy, or respect. Admittedly, I loved every stare and glare. Not only did I feel alive, but I looked alive too. Men half my age were coming on to me, and when I told them that I was old enough to be their mother, they told me they didn't believe. Some I'm sure were turned on by it, and some were gutted, as I *was* too old for them. Some knew but refused to let my age get in the way of them still turning on the charm and attempting to win me over! I had a distant memory that I was once addicted to drugs but one day I realised that all the things that had triggered me over the past 13 years had absolutely lost their power. What the hell was going on? My head could not comprehend the transformation.

Another time I recall in the supported accommodation I was in the kitchen making a drink and telling some of the other residents about my prison tactics, and Pauline walked into the kitchen whilst I was telling the others how I was clairvoyant and how I'd met a woman in jail who was a spiritualist who had told me about my grandmother who had passed away in April 2002. Pauline just looked at me but didn't say a word. I thought nothing of it (well, why should I?) and just continued to tell my stories. I'd later heard somewhere that Christians didn't believe in spiritualists, mediums, clairvoyants, and so on. The fact that I never charged anyone for a reading meant I wasn't operating in evil, didn't it? I also never gave bad news to people. Don't get me wrong; I warned them of situations and enemies and things to beware of, but I never revealed a death or a tragedy. I simply told them about their past, present, and future. I always closed each meeting with the Lord's Prayer. However, I did invoke spirits without fully understanding what I was doing. Some spirits seemed calm and friendly, and some seemed evil and angry. I was pinned down by spirits in bed a few times after doing a reading. The force was physical, but you don't see anyone there. The presence was heavy and very uncomfortable. Most of the time this happened, I was unable to talk as the spirit paralysed my mouth as I fought to say the Lord's Prayer. There were also times when I woke up in the middle of the night and there was a strong presence in my bed trying to get sexual with me, and that was so damn annoying! I used to get really vexed, and as soon as the strong hold let go, I'd curse and swear, and it would soon go as my fear switched to anger. But none of that stopped me from practicing clairvoyance. I really didn't understand the powers behind it. However, the Ouija board was something I'd never messed with; it had never appealed to me, and I knew from hearing other people's stories that things could get so serious that the only way to rid of the evil of the spirits invoked by the Ouija board was deliverance from a man or woman of God. No one ever told me about the spirit realm; I was taught nothing, but I had an intuitive knowing and I knew how to access unseen powers. I just found myself telling a fellow inmate back in 1997 her past, present, and future. The only encounters I'd had with spiritualism were visiting a tarot card reader a few times when I worked in the betting shop back in 1992–95 and having a reading done by a clairvoyant just before I went to HMP Brockhill in 1996. However, I couldn't read everyone, as I believed some people had a barrier so you can't get in. The secrets of invoking such spirits were revealed to me by the devil himself, when I say the devil, I am suggesting negative thoughts and negative voices, so when I say that I was not taught by a person or that I had not read some information on the spirit realm, I knew absolutely nothing except from an inward guiding. No man or woman had informed me how to practice sorcery. It was because I had been taught by the devil himself that I was able to intrude on peoples' hidden secrets.

I recall one day leaving my room in the supported accommodation and walking toward the living-room. I had to walk past the main office on my way. As I neared the office, Pauline was standing outside. I greeted her and then found myself saying that I would come to church on Sunday. As soon as the words were out, I could have kicked myself. I remember thinking to myself, "What did you say that for, you fool!" But I am a woman of my word who doesn't like to go back on it without a good reason, so church it was on Sunday! This conversation took place early in the week. Later, that week, I received a letter from Mommy (the lady who prayed for me before I left prison). The letter was full of hope and plenty of well-wishing. Also, in the letter she told me to read some scriptures from the Bible, Because I respected Mommy and I really liked her, I decided to find these scriptures and read them but I didn't know how to look for these chapters and verses, so I asked Pauline to help me to understand. Also living in the supported accommodation was a guy named Clive, who was a church member and had some knowledge of the Bible, so he showed me how to look for chapters and verses. After going through the Bible and reading the verses from the chapters I'd been given by Mommy, I really didn't have a clue what they were on about. There's absolutely nothing wrong with my reading and writing skills, and I understand life itself, but this Bible I could not understand. Mommy also wrote about ten Psalms for me to read at night before I went to sleep, but the only one I was at all familiar with was Psalm 23. I only knew the first two lines: "The Lord is my shepherd; I shall not want."

Sunday of that week came much quicker than I wished. Fortunately, the service didn't start until 1.30 p.m., so I'd have plenty of time to hit the shops before church. Sunday was my best day for shoplifting by far. Although the main stores and fashion shops didn't open until 11 a.m. on Sunday, it was my most profitable day. So, I planned to hit the shops as early as possible, sell the goods, and then return to the supported accommodation with my cash. Then I'd go to church. Even though I didn't believe in going to church, I wouldn't go to church and then go shoplifting. I believed that was a bad omen. So, I got up that morning, and as I was planning what shops to hit and where to go, something came over me. I remember feeling lethargic. I had no energy, no get-up-and-go, no oomph! I really can't explain what exactly came over me that day. Suddenly, when it was almost noon, I started to feel a bit more energetic. It was far too late to go out grafting now and get back on time for church, so I just put it down to a gut feeling that maybe I shouldn't be going out that particular day. Although I'd said I was attending church, I planned to stay for an hour, and then I was getting out of there!

I arrived at church at 1.30. I had been warned by a couple of the residents that the Pastor was Pauline's husband, was very boring. One resident told me that she felt that even God Himself fell asleep when the Pastor preached! I can honestly say that it wasn't as bad as I expected, but I wasn't going back in a hurry. So, what was said in church that day? Well, the Pastor told us a story about a man who gave his wife a to-do lists every day. This wasn't just some ordinary list; it was very important, because if she had ten things to do that day but only managed to do seven or even nine of them, then in his eyes she had failed her to-do-list. I didn't understand the parable and didn't dare to ask, as everyone else in the congregation seemed to understand what the Pastor was saying, and I didn't want to appear to be stupid. I kept quiet and left it at that. The Pastor also mentioned how to hear directly from God. Yes, how to hear God's voice! He mentioned the four keys to hearing from God and told us to write them down. I thought to myself, "I don't need to write this down; I'll remember these four keys." Before I got back to the supported accommodation, I had forgotten them. I recall thinking that I could always ask Pauline if I really wanted to know, as she came to the supported accommodation every day. What else did I think about church? Well, let me put it this way: I wouldn't be rushing back there in a hurry! The following Sunday came around pretty quick. To this day, I don't know what made me go back to church. All I know is that I'd stopped taking drugs and was now having a drink every night, as there were a few service users who were alcohol dependent at the supported accommodation. It was quite an eye-opener, really, that I'd started to drink almost every night. Don't get me wrong; I've drunk alcohol in the past and quite enjoyed the feeling and the taste of certain spirits. However, never before had I drank alcohol to get drunk; I had only drunk it to be sociable. Now it was as if I had a time limit and had to get it down my throat quickly. It never occurred to me that a lot of former heroin addicts use another drug or alcohol as a substitute. So why am I telling you this? I believe I went through this experience to show me that I was not at all in control of drugs or alcohol! I truly believe that God used this knowledge to grip me with His mighty hand and lead me to church, because I never wanted to go back. I planned to go shoplifting again the second week I had a pain in my neck which made it stiff, but it wouldn't have stopped me from doing what I wanted to do, which was to go out and graft. So, there I was in church with a slight pain in my neck and a face on me like a wet weekend in Brighton! The Pastor began to preach the word from the Bible and all of a sudden, he looked straight into my eyes as if he was speaking to my soul and said something that gripped me with fear! He was talking about what losing your conscience is like. "It's like having a deep cut on your arm. It hurts at first and can be quite painful. But if you keep prodding at that wound, it eventually becomes numb." That's what had happened to me! I recall thinking, "Oh my God! How can this be mended?" He also went back to the to-do list parable he had spoken about previously. The woman in the story represented human beings. Her husband represented God. The to-do list was the Ten Commandments. So, I had to keep all the Ten Commandments to do God's will? Well, that was my salvation out of the window! Because according to what the Pastor was saying, I had broken all ten! But what this man of God was saying was that even if you break only one commandment and diligently carry out the remaining nine, you are not obeying God's Ten Commandments. A lot of people think that if you do not murder and have no other gods, then you are safe; that is what I thought too at the time. I thought if you broke one or two, such as by telling a lie, you were not as bad as someone who had broken all ten. What am I trying to say? To do God's will we must obey the Ten Commandments as a package. If we lie, then we are no better than a thief or a murderer. He also went on about the four keys to hearing God's voice. This time I wrote them down so as not to forget. The Pastor also said that we should always ask God if what we had been taught in church that day was true. What freaked me out more than anything on this day was the way the Pastor looked into my eyes. He knew my name, as he was married to Pauline, but she did not know what I was doing daily. In fact, he knew nothing about me. I concluded that the message in church that day was definitely for me. After the service, Pauline walked over to the congregation and spoke to each one of us. When she greeted me, she asked how I was? Instantly, the drama queen came right up to the surface. I told her that my neck was a little stiff and laid it on so thick that even I felt sorry for me! Suddenly, she laid her hands on me and began to pray and she said she would speak to the spirit that was causing the pain. To my absolute surprise, when she finished praying, she looked straight at me and said, "Jesus said there's nothing wrong with your neck!" She then walked away. I was gobsmacked! There was a slight pain, but she was right. I was overreacting; there was absolutely nothing wrong with my neck, as I'd have gone shoplifting with this little pain and thought nothing of it. She also took no time to confirm that the spirit in me didn't want me to be in the church. If I was perfectly honest, I had to agree. I just want to clarify that where I use the term spirit, it can also be likened to energy. Neither spirit or energy has form but has the capacity to be negative, positive or indifferent depending on the emotional field it is in.

Later, that night when I was in my room, I used the four keys to hear from God and asked Him if what was said in church that day was true. After a short while, He said to me, "Yes, most of it was the gospel." I then asked Him, "So how do I get my conscience back?" There was no answer. What I should say is that I didn't wait for the answer. I began to pray with an open heart and earnestly asked the Father to please mend this damaged and broken conscience of mine. I found myself opening my heart and telling Him all my wrongs and pouring all my troubles before Him. The last sentence was something like, "Father, I know you can hear me, so please answer my prayer, Lord, as I've come to you for compassion and forgiveness, amen." I felt as though a great weight was lifted off my shoulders. God never really stood a chance of getting a word in edgewise, as I just laid all my problems at His feet. After I prayed, I didn't wait for a response from God, but I knew deep, deep down that He had heard me and that I was not being ignored.

Clearing my conscience did play on my mind quite a bit. I suppose it was fear, because I knew deep down that you're not supposed to steal and lie to get through life, but these wrongs had taken me over and had become my way of life.

It was a Saturday morning, as I recall, and a mate of mine was out on a community visit from prison. We planned to meet early in the afternoon. I had told her that I'd get her some clothes, so I went shoplifting. I returned with a lot of goods for both of us, but I couldn't find it in me to charge her anything, as she was in prison and was like a daughter to me. We met, and I gave her the clothes. When she left, I decided to go out again, as I wanted some money; I was getting used to having money in my purse to buy what I wanted. I entered a designer shop and took two or three jackets (one was worth £500.00) into the changing room where no one could see me. I began to do my thing, but then my phone started to ring. It startled me, as this shop was situated in the city centre in a shopping mall where I'd always had trouble getting reception on my phone. I recall looking at my phone and it had no signal but it kept on ringing. I looked at my phone to see who was calling. It was Pauline I tried to continue to steal, but I couldn't carry on. I felt guilty. I would have earned a tidy sum if I'd have successfully stolen this coat, but I just couldn't do it, especially with Pauline on the other end of my phone. I decided to leave the shop empty-handed. Pauline had called for a general chat. I found myself asking her if she wanted a hand running the supported accommodation. She said we would talk about it when she was in on Monday, but we spoke after the church service on Sunday instead. We talked for a little while, and she explained that she would allow me to help run the house as a volunteer, which suited me. At last, someone who was totally aware of my criminal record and past was giving me a chance! I started work in the house. I told myself that I needed a few quid to see me through until I got my benefits sorted, so I planned to go out one last time to steal before I committed to helping out in the supported accommodation. As I got ready, I planned what shops to go to. Just as I was about to leave, my conscience kicked in, and I recall thinking, "I can't work with people who have recently been released from jail and go shoplifting." I also couldn't do that to Pauline as she was giving me a chance. This woman was giving me an opportunity to get a grip on my life, but what was I going to do for money? I had become accustomed to always having money in my purse. I found myself sitting down on my bed and praying to God for help and advice. I recall asking God what should I do? I recall saying that I am not asking Him for money, but how will I earn money? Now that I'd taken that big step in asking God for help, how was I going to cope financially? I'd admitted that I could not go out and steal any more because I felt guilty, and it was not because of fear of being caught that was stopping me. Although Pauline was willing to take a big chance on me, this position was a voluntary job, which meant I would work for nothing, although I would eventually receive benefits. My criminal record was terrible. I had over fifty offences and twenty-nine convictions, and I had lost count of how much time I'd spent behind a steel door looking at prison walls. I had now confessed that I knew what I was doing was wrong, but I had never lived on benefits in the past I had always felt that I had to steal to survive, as Job Seekers Allowance was something like £65.00 per week. I also knew I wouldn't get the full amount of benefits because of the number of crisis loans I'd had over the years which would be deducted from my weekly entitlement, so how was I going to cope? I was also in a bit of a predicament, as I was waiting for my current application for benefits to be processed. I really wanted to send a couple of the girls whom I'd met on my last jail sentence some clothes and money, as I knew what it was like to be in jail and finding it a bit tough. The problems kept on flooding my mind. I knew I'd be tempted to steal, because it was what I did as a way of life, and although I was willing to try to change, I also knew it wasn't going to be easy. A couple of days later, I heard from some of the girls who were still doing their time, and the urge to go out and get them something was too strong. I spoke to God again, and this time I went before Him with justification in my heart to see if He would understand that I was contemplating to steal but for a valid reason. All I wanted was to be able to go and graft a few quid to see myself all right, to get a few things for one of the girls, and to have enough money to be able to post the clothes to my friend in prison. So, I got ready to go out, and as I was almost out of the door of my room, I felt something tug at my heart. Because I'd been on drugs for such a long time, my feelings and emotions were usually totally numb, so when I felt this tug on my heartstrings, it jolted me to face God, because what I was about to do was not right. Even though I could sort of justify my intentions, theft is theft, and "thou shall not steal" is a commandment and not a suggestion. I deflated and sat on the edge of my bed and began saying a silent prayer to God. "What shall I do, Lord? I'm not asking you for money, because although I don't really know you, something inside of me knows that to ask God for money is a very bad omen. What I want to know, Lord, is what do I do? Please help me, Father; please give me the solution to this major problem." I was sat waiting for an answer from God when my door opened and in walked Pauline I recall looking at her and thinking, "Why has she just walked into my room?" but I couldn't say anything, as I was totally gobsmacked. She had never walked into my room without knocking and waiting for a reply, so why had she just walked straight into to my room this day? Before I could say anything, she looked at me and said, "God told me to come and give you this." In her hand was some money. My mouth was open, and I was totally freaked out. I thought it was a set-up! I started scanning the room for CCTV but soon realised that there wasn't any sort of camera's hidden anywhere, and even if there had been, cameras cannot read your mind, and I had prayed silently in my mind. I sat in amazement and wonder. I looked at the money and then back up to the ceiling as if looking at God and back to the money again, as I couldn't believe what was happening. I kept saying to myself in my mind "God is my provider".

CHAPTER 8

DIVORCING THE DEVIL

After I'd been working at the supported accommodation for a couple of weeks, I started to change. I wasn't the same woman who had walked through the supported accommodation doors in January. Pauline gave me lots of advice on doing my job, and we developed a good relationship. She used to call me into her office or the conference room for a chat and to pray for me, and sometimes she would tell me about things that had happened to me in the past and things that were to come in the future. I told her how I'd got into practicing clairvoyance and that it came very natural for me to sit down with people and just start telling them about their lives. Pauline however, told me that what I was doing was dealing with evil spirits which explained why I sometimes got attacked after doing a reading with a client. Whenever she spoke to people concerning their pasts and futures, she always told them what she believed God had told her to say. Basically, she was highly intuitive and this is what she meant by hearing from God. One day we were in the conference room talking and she became very spiritual and said to me, "God told me to tell you that you were married to the devil." The words were said with conviction, and because of the life I had led, I knew it was a message from God as it resonated with my intuition. She also had mentioned to me a few weeks before that I had to be very careful when speaking to God always to make sure I was in God's presence before I opened my mouth to speak, as the devil (negativity) wanted me back badly and would creep in whilst I was praying to God, and that was quite scary. I asked her, "How will I know God's presence?" She said, "You'll know," and smiled at me. I knew she was very spiritual because of the things she'd said to me and to others in the house. I never told her the specifics of the drug addiction and drug abuse, my ex-partner, the life I'd led, and so on. She was always spot on, never wavering or trying to guess about my life. Nor did she ask any questions; she told it like it was. She also said to me that she knew I was very spiritual because she had heard me telling the other residents about my tactics with clairvoyance. She went on to tell me that I was not clairvoyant; I was a child of God. A child of God hears directly from God. God speaks to all His children, but He gave me a gift to foresee and to speak His word. I knew that was true, because God had told me to tell Pauline something a couple of days before this conversation, and I had delivered the message and watched as God revealed Himself to me and Pauline. She also told me that I would not become a drug worker which is what I wanted at the time because of my experience. That was the only thing I believed she had got wrong, as I was on a mission to counsel other users because of the lifestyle I'd led for many years. I knew so much about the lifestyle that I thought I would be able to relate to other people in that situation. It's also a known fact that some of the best drug workers are former addicts. What I didn't realise at the time was that to be a drug worker you may have to offer an alternative legal drug to replace the illegal drug, or at least you have to support that way of coming off class A substances and as I know from experience, the alternative drugs don't work the way God does. I cannot offer drug users a substitute drug. I began to let the phrase "married to the devil" penetrate my mind. All the bad things I'd done in life were swimming around in my head. I'd stolen, lied, dishonoured my parents, committed crimes on the Sabbath rather than serving God, committed adultery, and the list went on and on. I knew that I had already asked for forgiveness but the thoughts bombarded my mind. Surely if God said I was married to the devil, then I must have been. I began to feel sick with dread that God Himself would have His work cut out with me! I then did what I'd learned to do best and pushed the thought to the back of my mind. That bit of information was too deep to sit and ponder on for too long.

Later that night, I was sitting in the living-room watching TV with Elaine. Suddenly, my whole body seem to be on fire. I was itching from the crown of my head to the soles of my feet. For the past few months, I'd suffered this itching all over my body periodically but had not found out what was causing it. But on this night, it went to another level. I felt as though I really was on fire. I'd been to my GP about this itching, and he had prescribed some shower gel and some cream to stop the itching, but I'd not used it as yet, as the problem had subsided. Typical. I was sat scratching like a madwoman, but I didn't want to go to my room and apply the cream. I suppose I thought it would calm down and then I could watch my soaps in peace. Elaine turned to me and said, "Why don't you try out the shower gel you got off your doctor?" She was right. I went to my room, and by the time I got there I felt like screaming; it was getting unbearable. I began to remove my clothes quickly and decided to get in the shower and use the gel. Then, once out of the shower, I'd use the cream to prevent further itching. I put my dressing-gown on and grabbed the shower gel, my towel, flip-flops, etc. I was just about to go to the communal showers when I plonked myself onto my bed and looked up toward ceiling. My itching stopped as quickly as it had started. I clasped my hands together, closed my eyes, and found myself asking God, "What do I need to do to divorce the devil?" I didn't expect to hear what God said to me next; nor did I want to believe that I'd heard my intuition speak! His voice was cool but firm and brooked no argument. He said, "You know what you have to do." I immediately opened my eyes and looked around my room. At that moment I felt dread and great sorrow. I recall saying, "No, God. Please, no!" My intuition didn't say anything more. He went silent, but I visualized Him sitting on His throne with His arms outstretched as if to say, "You asked, and I answered." I then began to obey the voice of God my intuition. As I looked around my room, everything looked different, tainted. I didn't realise it at that time, but God had opened my eyes. The enormity of what I had been told to do sank in, and I couldn't pretend that I didn't know what I had to do. I stood up and walked over to my wardrobe. I opened the doors, and all my worldly belongings seemed to look back at me. I saw all my lovely clothes I had acquired with ill-gotten money or stolen them from the shop. I slowly took my jeans out of the wardrobe and grieved as the realisation hit me. I remember taking my least popular jeans out first, as getting rid of them wouldn't hurt as much. The devil was creeping back in to my mind and I realised that if I held back anything, even so much as a vest top, then there was no point in doing what I knew needed to be done. I shrugged the negative thoughts off and began to take all my clothes out of the wardrobe. There were piles of clothes, and there were some that I'd never got a chance to wear that had price tags still on them. I then looked at my Ugg boots and Ugg scarf that I loved so much, but like I said, there was no point in just getting rid of a few things. No, this was a divorce, not a trial separation. After I cleared all my underwear, clothes, pyjamas, coat's, jewellery, trainers, shoes, toiletries, perfumes, hair extensions, and cleaning fluids, I sat on my bed like a little girl waiting for the next instruction from God. He told me to put them in large, see-through bin liners and then He would give me my next instruction. I had a few see-through bin liners in a drawer in my room, so used them to put my things in. I was completely stripped. My make-up was ill-gotten as well, as were all my hair products. It would be fair to say that the only thing in that room that was not ill-gotten was one old dressing-gown that my mom had given me a while back, some flip-flops that I had kept from a jail sentence, a pair of cream-coloured stretch jeans I'd never worn, and a brown floral top. I also had a couple of pairs of knickers that weren't stolen and one or two bras. Once I'd packed everything into the bags—and there were a few bags, I can tell you! —I sat and waited for the next instruction. I believe the Holy Spirit led me to do what I did next. It was still the voice of God, but it came from within, and it was gentle and calm. I did not have any control over the next instruction. It was now past midnight, and everyone had gone to their rooms. I walked as if in a trance to the kitchen and opened the door which led to the back garden and began to place all the bags outside. Not once was I scared and not once did I stop to think of the danger of being outside in the dark alone because I instinctively knew that I was walking with a power far greater than anything I had ever experienced. As I went to and from my room carrying the bags, I realised that I was still wearing my glasses, which had also been paid for with stolen money, and my mobile phone too. I quickly put my contact lenses into a bag with the solution I used to clean them, my mobile phone, and my glasses. After I took the final bag out of my room and to the garden, I locked the kitchen area and began to walk through the living-room to my room. As I was walking, I heard a load groan coming from behind me. I stopped dead in my tracks and looked over my shoulder. As I went to continue to walk towards my room, I distinctively heard the same deep, gut-wrenching groan again! This time I stood tall, threw my shoulders back, held my head high, and took one final look over my shoulder to let the devil know I had heard him but was not about to entertain him with argument, conversation, or fear. I smiled and carried on back to my room. I couldn't believe what had taken place in a few hours. I called Pauline and because she was the one who walked into my room with the money that day after my prayer to God, I thought she should know what had happened that night. She was shocked when I told her, and she said that she had wondered why God had told her to take me shopping that weekend. She also asked what I was doing with the clothes and offered to take them to a charity shop, but I told her that God had told me to put them in the back garden for the night, and in the morning, I was to put them on the street and leave them and walk away. It was a very emotional conversation, and I realised just how much this woman meant to me.

The following morning, I woke up and looked out of my bedroom window and saw all my stuff neatly packed up in the back garden. I didn't feel too bad, as it goes. I quickly went into the kitchen, and there I found Johnny, the house security guard and caretaker. I asked him to give me a hand with putting the bags of clothes and other stuff on the road next to the supported accommodation. I didn't want any of the residents to bring anything from the bags back into the house. As far as I was concerned, this was going to be the last time I ever set eyes on my belongings. I felt I needed to explain what I'd done and why I'd done it to Elaine, as I knew she'd understand and respect why I couldn't give my belongings to my family or friends. The fact that they had all been acquired through criminal activity meant that if I had personally given them to people, then it would not have been a complete separation. I also believed that I would be passing my tainted goods over to them, and that could be seen as passing a curse over to them. I also felt that because they were ill-gotten, I wanted nothing more to do with them. I wasn't about to give them to anyone because of what they stood for. No, I had to tell her that they could not return into this house for specific reasons. It didn't take long for a couple of the other residents to discover that there was a load of new clothes and belongings on the street. When I told them that they had belonged to me and that they must not under any circumstances bring anything from the bags back onto

69

the premises, some of them thought I'd gone completely mad. It wasn't just the residents that thought I'd gone too far with this "God thing." as they all termed it. My mom was very surprised and thought that Pauline had put me up to it. I was hurt to think that my mom would think anyone could talk me into doing something so drastic, especially as I'd started to find the real me! The fact that I was no longer trapped by the devil which meant victory for me and the beginning of getting to know who I really was on this earth. The purpose for which I had been created was starting to dawn on me.

After my divorce to the devil, I sat in my room having conversations with God morning, noon, and night. God opened the eyes of my understanding and taught me how to read the Bible. Every day when I woke up, I asked God, "What am I to do today, Lord?" He spoke to me in my intuition and instructed me, and sometimes He led me to scriptures in the Bible which told me what I wanted to know. The way God moves is awesome.

The church I joined in 2011, was founded by an Apostle based on a vision he had whilst in the presence of God (2 Corinthians 3:17, Luke 4:18–19). Pauline often travelled down to London to the church headquarters. On one trip, I went with her, as she wanted me to give my testimony. I'd also have the pleasure of meeting the Apostle. We sat in the congregation whilst the apostle preached the word of God. He then handed the microphone over to Pauline, who introduced me, and I stood and gave my testimony. I must stress that before I went up to speak in front of all these strangers to proclaim that I was a drug addict and a thief before Jesus took me out of the lions' den, I was extremely nervous and felt couldn't do it alone. I looked up towards heaven and whispered, "Help me to do this, Lord. I depend on You." Before I knew it, I found Pauline standing with me in front of many people. I had an unction that made me bold and fearless. I knew that the Holy Spirit (the voice of my intuition) took over, and I gave my testimony to about fifty strangers. After my speech, the apostle laid his hands on me and prayed. I recall hearing all the congregation praying in tongues, and the next thing I knew I was on the floor. I was shocked. I felt as though I was being pushed, and I tried to fight it. In the end I gave up. I fell flat on the floor and couldn't get up. I felt strange. Eventually, after around ten minutes, I stood and walked back to my seat.

After I stepped down off the pulpit, I went and sat with the congregation, and there was a finger buffet for everyone. I sat with Pauline by the entrance to where the food was laid out. Basically, you had to pass Pauline and me to get to the food. Everyone made their way towards the buffet. Most of the church members greeted me and said that I had given a powerful testimony and shook my hand and said, "God bless you", but some of them seemed angry and ignored me. I wasn't bothered in the slightest, but I was annoyed at their ignorance. "Why are these people angry with me?" I thought. "Surely this testimony signifies that the God they serve is a living God and miracles happen today!; why are they not rejoicing?"

A Note from The Author

I would like to clarify who I believe God is.
God is an unseen power which has no form.
God can not be created nor can He be destroyed.
God speaks to us ALL through our intuition. If we are not trained to hear or identify the voice of our intuition, you may meet someone who clearly hears their intuition and they can deliver a message from God to you.
We all have an intuition and some of us are highly intuitive.
God is a religious word for;
The universe,
unseen power,
higher self,
energy
The Self
and many other words that we relate to a powerful force. When I say I feel God's presence, I am also saying that I feel a powerful force of love and acceptance within and around me. When I say I hear God's voice, I am referring to hearing my intuition speak.

Word hit the street, and quite a few people heard that I'd moved on by taking such a big step. Some thought it was a phase I was going through; others admired the fact that I'd truly done some soul-searching. Some were pleased to see that I was no longer committing crime or taking drugs and consequently was no longer being thrown into prison. One of my aunts (my mom's sister) brought me a lot of really nice clothes that she hadn't worn along with some she had worn but had taken good care of. Pauline went shopping and bought me a lot of nice jewellery and underwear and tops, and she also put clothes in carrier bags and brought them to the supported accommodation and told me to have what I wanted. She also said if there was anything that was too big or not my style, I was to leave them in the bags, and she would collect them back from me. My wardrobe was looking healthy again. I did not miss any of the items I had got rid of. That is a big puzzle to me, I must confess.

CHAPTER 9

WHAT DRUGS CAN DO TO A SOUL (YOUR MIND, WILL, AND EMOTIONS)

I'm not going to say that any of this was easy, because life isn't easy. All I know is that since I came out of prison, I can honestly say that I have been gripped by God's Grace and love. When I was taking drugs and committing crime, I often used to think that no one couldn't save me, as I'd done too much wrong in my life. I used to think that God does not forgive us for all our sins. I also thought that God was a force and a power outside of us but that's not true. God is our intuition which is in our subconscious mind or what is known as the heart of man. I also recall taking hundreds of pounds worth of class A drugs and not wanting to wake up the next day. I really didn't want to live most days, as my days on this earth consisted of drugs for breakfast, trying to survive through the day—I suppose I could call that lunch, more drugs for dinner, and then even more drugs for supper. I sit back and think of the places I've visited because I was vulnerable and it seems as though the drugs had full control of my life. I walked the streets for hours some nights lonely and cold with nowhere to go. Lots of my drug associates were only too glad to have me stay over at their places, because

I used to give them drugs in payment for the privilege of sleeping on their sofas for the night. Sometimes I used to test them by telling them that I didn't have any money or drugs when I asked if it was OK for me to stay on the sofa until the morning. Some of these associates grudgingly let me stay, believing I had nothing except the clothes I was wearing. I suppose they were thinking of the money I would earn the next day. At least they were going to get some drugs then! Some were so blatant that when I asked if I could stay for the night, they made up some cock-and-bull story and made excuses, but when I pulled out my stash of drugs, the tune changed in a nanosecond. I had heard of other drug users leaving their peers to die when they had overdosed. Some would watch their friend lying on the floor unconscious and rather than call an ambulance, some would rifle through the pockets, steal what they could and leave their friend to die. I recall watching a couple empty the pockets of one of their relative s who had overdosed and collapsed in the street. I waited and called the paramedics for this man. The things I heard and witnessed were soul destroying.

I should also share a story about the time I was living in London with Darren. We were waiting to score drugs in a drug user's flat. I sat with Darren as we waited for the dealer. A woman was also there with two of her brothers. She was an enemy of mine, and I couldn't stand the sight of her. She'd only been out of jail a couple of days and was still celebrating her freedom with her brothers. The dealer arrived, and we all scored our drugs. I felt like I was going to pass out and collapse from rattling (another word for detoxing). As I got my foil plate ready for a much-needed smoke, I saw my enemy and her two brothers cooking up their gear on a metal spoon and ready to inject. I'd never injected heroin before and had never been drawn to this way of taking heroin. There was also another woman in the flat who was just about to inject the heroin into her groin. I'd never seen anything like it before and felt really sick. All of a sudden, I noticed that the woman whom I regarded as an enemy was lying on the floor and her lips were going blue. To this day I don't know what came over me; it must have been God. I was horrified but very calm as I informed the people in the flat that she had overdosed. They all looked at me and then at her body on the dirty floor, and to my shock and horror, they were more interested in having their hit than in helping her! Her two brothers were more interested in getting the needle in their veins than helping their sister, who was at death's door!! At this point I was almost

74

throwing up due to an intense rattle. I calmly put my foil down and felt her pulse. She had stopped breathing. Remaining calm, I made a circle with my index finger and thumb and placed it as a barrier on her lips. I then placed my lips on the circle I'd made with my finger and thumb and began to give her the kiss of life. I'd never done this before, but my main concern was to blow life back into this woman's lungs. I did this a few times and proceeded to pump at her heart. I did this for about two or three minutes, but it felt like a lot longer. No one else seemed interested. They were more interested in their fix, her own brothers included. She coughed at long last and came back to life. I thanked God. I was then overcome with love for this woman, and all animosity went out the window. After a while she thanked me, and it came to light that she had paid for the drugs that her brothers and this other woman were too busy with to care about her dying! We became drug mates, and the next day she took me out grafting with her, as she was what's known as a kiter (someone who uses stolen credit cards in shops and stores and forges the signature of the true owner to obtain money and goods by deception). We were supposed to split the money 50-50, but she paid her brother more than me and all he'd done was tag along. I didn't go out with her again after that, but it showed me that in this dark life you either wise up and swim or you drown. After what I'd seen, I became a swimmer of an Olympic standard going for the gold medal. I saved her life whilst her brothers stood by and were more interested in saving what was in a needle, and after all that, she ripped me off! The drugs are that powerful. They controlled everything—the lifestyle, the food you ate or didn't eat, and the thoughts that went through your mind. When I was on drugs, I never liked other drug users even though I was probably more devious than them. It's only now that I have the love of God in my life that I have come to realise that drugs have a powerful spirit behind them. The drug has full control whether the person realises or not. How many times have I heard people say, "I can control my habit"? how many times did I say it and truly believe it? I lost count. Crack cocaine lifted me up so high that I was puffed up with arrogance and pride. I felt like a giant in the drug den. Some people would literally do anything you told them to once you had that powerful powder in your hand. You had the drugs in your right hand and the drug users' dignity in your left. Because I grafted for my own drugs, the praise for my style, even to my own ears, was very embarrassing. People would tell me what they thought I wanted to hear in order to get me to sort them out with my drugs. In reality, they just belittled themselves before me and my drugs and I knew they were trying to manipulate me in to thinking they actually meant it. Personally, I could never beg anyone for drugs; I would give them a lot of patter (manipulating talk), but I wouldn't beg.

I would then take heroin to bring me down, as the high isn't always nice when you've smoked too much crack. What a dangerous place to be, day in, and day out! No wonder prison was a welcoming place of rest for my soul.

Can you imagine waking up one morning after you have had a strong addiction for almost thirteen years, opening your eyes, and not knowing that you have been delivered from such a powerful thing? I'd tried loads of times to come off drugs. I'd tried with the aid of prescribed drugs and cold turkey. I even thought I could do it by monitoring how much I was taking and cutting down. I failed every time. I called out in the pit of my soul for help, but I thought it was a useless thing, as no one could hear me. I used to tell myself, "One day I'm going to get off the drugs and be someone successful" The truth is I never believed it but I always felt the urge to affirm it. The cry for help was inside my head. I would smile on the outside or tell people I was fine, but inside I felt as though I was dead, beyond repair, heading to the pits of hell; and I couldn't wait to get there, because surely it would be better than living this sorry life.

The drugs don't just destroy your soul; they destroy your life. I knew a few people who died because of drugs, and the devastation they left behind no amount of crying could mend. Drugs are evil and are a way to self-destruction. It's not just the person who takes the drug who's affected; his or her family and true friends feel the pressure that living a drug-fuelled life brings. I've often described drug addicts as victims of a very cruel addiction and disease.

I certainly made a lot of mistakes. Once I got caught shoplifting, and because I was rattling and really didn't want to spend a weekend in the local police station, I gave my younger sister's name as my alias. Another time I used the name of my friend Laura. Both women were angry with me. There were times I was sold out to the drugs, and I haven't met a user who never crossed that invisible line. If they never had the bottle to do such things, they certainly thought about it.

CHAPTER 10

FINDING JESUS CHRIST

When I use to hear Christians talk about Jesus, I never knew why they called Him the Lord. I did not grow up knowing the bible or going to church so Christianity was alien to me. When I looked in to becoming a Muslim, I experienced confusion when praying as I felt that I wanted to speak to God and express my feelings and the pain that was locked up in my soul but I was only showed how to do the prayers and I was aware of fasting. Now, I'm not here to give readers a religious lesson nor am I qualified to do so but what I can share with you is the love that I have in my heart for my intuition which is also known as God or what the Bible refers to as the Holy Spirit. I feel His presence when I pray to Him, when I worship Him, and when I lay all my worries and cares at His feet. He comforts and gently guides me. I have His promise that He will not leave me nor forsake me (Hebrews 13:5). There is nothing too big or too small for Him. He is mighty, merciful, and compassionate, and I call upon Him in my hour of need. Through studying the Bible I have come to discover that Jesus was a man and He was led by His intuition. Our intuition is what the Bible refers to as Christ and because Jesus was completely surrendered to His intuition and because His intuition led him to perform miracles, heal the sick and walk in wisdom, His intuition (God the Christ) was more significant that Jesus' physical form. This is why Jesus could say "I and my Father are One" Jesus is the embodiment of the Christ (Pure intuition and stillness) when I look back at all the times when I felt protection from within, I now realise it was God within me. I believed miracles only happened when Jesus was physically on earth, and now that He was gone, I thought miracles were non-existent. Forgive me for preaching, but the love I have for God in my heart is a very powerful feeling. I am humbled by this revelation as my intuition was louder than my old conditioned mind. The old conditioned mind with all of its destructive programs was silenced by my powerful intuition known as God because He not only took the drugs out of my life but swiftly removed the damage they had done to my brain, the damage that surgery could not fix. It is a fact someone who's been hooked on heroin and crack for such a long time may physically come off the drug, but mentally it may be impossible. I hear so many ex-addicts talk about their daily fight to stay clean so are technically still in bondage to the drugs. There has not been a day to date when I have had the urge to smoke drugs. I have no triggers. (A trigger is a situation or image that can cause an addict to experience a craving for a drug. For example, if someone used to use tinfoil to smoke drugs, although they have come off the drug, when they see the foil, it triggers something in the brain, and immediately the drug comes back to the front of the mind which can make a person begin to crave drugs, or think about drugs) When I see foil, drugs don't spring to mind. When I see a small glass bottle, a plastic water bottle, an inhaler, or anything I once used as drug paraphernalia, it has absolutely no effect on me. I have also seen service users sneak drugs in the supported accommodation, I have come face-to-face with heroin and crack cocaine and it has absolutely no effect on me or my mind. I have been cured of such thoughts. That isn't the only damage I had; no, I was being eaten up inside by apathy, grief, fear, lust, anger, pride, hate, stealing, and lying—all the things that people endure whilst living deep in sin. It's no wonder I thought God didn't want to know the likes of me. God is intuition. God is not just some powerful force outside of us humans, He is the gentle, still voice that is in the heart of every man. Jesus is the power of God's word. Everything that God said, Jesus became this is why Jesus is called the Son of God. Jesus carried God's unfailing power (The Christ) in His physical form. Christ means God and this is why Jesus Christ was and is still being called God today.

I had a lot of demons destroying my soul. My understanding of how to live life was clouded by sin, (the true biblical meaning of sin simply means, man without God, or to simplify, man who cannot discern the voice of his own intuition and the ability to obey his intuition). When I heard people talk about demons, I used to think to myself, "You can't say something like that to someone; demons are monsters!" I used to see *demon* as a very insulting word, but now I know the truth. A demon is best described as a destructive thought pattern that sits in the subconscious mind. I used the knowledge of the Bible and personal development to understand and gain wisdom about life.

As you have read, I have now gained spiritual knowledge and the truth about who God is. God does forgive, and He certainly loves us all no matter what we've done or haven't done. Can we really comprehend our intuition not loving us? Can we comprehend our intuition holding a grudge against us? The love I have experienced from God is known as Agape which means unconditional love and acceptance. Now that I have allowed Jesus (Gods word in the Bible) to take control of my life, I now know that unconditional love is acceptance.

I'm at a place where I'm becoming dependent on God (the prompting, leading and voice of my intuition) for my life. I am learning how to abide in Christ, in other words, I am learning how to discern my intuition. Yes, I still make mistakes and some poor decisions but as long as I know that there is a love deep within me that is willing to guide and protect me, I now take life a lot easier as I have an assurance that my intuition never fails me. The hardest part for me was learning to let ill feelings go. Submitting to God and yielding to forgiveness is a learning curve. Getting my head around what God has done in my life is a big thing, and I can say that I never played a part in it. All the power and the glory belong to God. The easy part of my walk nowadays is the daily worship, praising to God and speaking to Him through prayer. Our intuition is powerful and all knowing and so learning to abide in Christ is possible if we have the desire to do so. A continuous practice in this manner is yielding a fruitful result in my life. As the Apostle Paul said, "I die daily" (1 Corinthians15:31). I have realised that I am dying to my old sinful ways daily and this is achieved by me studying the bible and personal development to continue to change my old mindset.

As I sit and write this true story, I realise that God is my all. My mom and others have said that they believe I have gone from one addiction to another. When I first heard that I was taken aback a bit, but my attitude towards God is devotion, not addiction. The difference is that when I was addicted, I *had* to have my drugs; I *needed* to have my drugs, because I was addicted to them, I now have a desire and yearning to know God and, I also *want* to have God. I enjoy having God, and I could not live without God. The fruits of the Holy Spirit are supernatural. They are love, joy, peace, patience, kindness, gentleness, goodness, faithfulness, and self-control (Galatians 5:22). Abiding in Christ (paying attention to our intuition and following His lead) is the only way that we may genuinely bear such fruit.

In the next chapter, I will talk about how I fell away from God. In ignorance, I allowed pride to enter my heart and so I could not discern the voice of my intuition. I think It is important that I share this with you, as many people allow pride to creep in to our hearts through ignorance. I got too comfortable with the knowledge that God loves me and I suppose I took it for granted that I am now saved from a life of destruction. The most important thing about falling or stumbling when walking a Christian walk is getting up again. If you fall or stumble a thousand times, get back up a thousand and one times. Repentance is a must if we're to have fellowship with the Lord. We can ask Him to show us the right way, the only way. The fact that we are saved by the grace of God is enough for us to recognise the love of our Father in heaven.

CHAPTER 11

THE BIG FALL FROM GOD

To remain diligent and study the Bible daily was challenging for me some days. Living and volunteering in the supported accommodation was not easy and I found that I could be easily distracted by some of the other service users. In my previous chapter I quoted that I died daily to my old habits and behaviours because, although I experienced an overnight transformation from drugs, destruction and a life of hell, I had to be committed to transforming my mind. When I first realised that God was real because of the miracle He performed in my life, I sort of took it for granted that God loved me, so I was free. Yes, I am free from inner bondage (Galatians 5:1), but that did not mean that God was about to change my thinking for me. I did not realise this at the time but it is so important to remain rooted and committed to this new lifestyle. I began to relax and by doing so, through ignorance, I allowed pride to go in to my subconscious mind. This was not wilful but pride it happened to me.

After I'd been saved and was living a clean life, I was running the supported accommodation as a volunteer support worker and managing the house by making sure the other residents were aware of all the house rules and I supported their support needs. Because of my responsibilities as a house leader and support worker, I had to be alert. As some of the other residents were in the same predicament as I had been when I first arrived at the house, I was able to sit down and tell them where I'd been and that there was a future for everyone. I didn't go around Bible-thumping or quoting words from the Bible; I simply told them how God had changed me and my life. It gave a few residents a glimmer of hope when they heard that my criminal record was much bigger than theirs and my drug life had been very bad. I never once hid anything from anyone, as I didn't feel I needed to. As time went by, I had dealings with the West Midlands and Staffordshire Probation Service, police officers, and service user charities (BLUE PILOT support team and Killway Housing). The reason I had dealings with those organizations was that I was a volunteer support worker. I supported some of the residents who had support needs, and I also supported them by prompting their appointments, and on a few occasions, I had to go along with a client to the doctor, dentist, or even shopping if they needed the additional support due to their identified support needs. All in all, I enjoyed my job, as it was something constructive, and I felt that I was putting something back into the community. Dealings with the police were an everyday occurrence, as they came to the supported accommodation to monitor one of the residents who was on a curfew and who had to be at his home address between 7 p.m. to 7a.m. As a volunteer support worker, I was asked by Pauline to answer the door when anyone called, and I introduced myself as a volunteer support worker when asked. I always told the residents it was up to them how to handle being on police bail, probation, or curfew. I made the residents aware that I would not volunteer information but I also cannot cover up for them if they breached any bail conditions. I would give the residents all the support they needed. Some residents didn't like the fact that I was no longer criminal-minded, some didn't believe that I no longer thought like a criminal, and some really didn't understand. When I had any spare time on my hands, I went to my room and spent it reading the Bible, praying, and building up a relationship with my intuition. As I'd got rid of my glasses, I sometimes asked God when I would get my eyesight back, but as I believed by faith that He would restore what I'd lost, I wasn't stressing over it.

Five weeks after I got rid of all my ill-gotten belongings, I had a slight headache from trying to read the Bible, as it was irritating my eyes. I had the money to go to the optician and buy some disposable contact lenses, but something drew me to begin to pray and ask God to give me my eyesight back. I remember placing my hands on my forehead and pleading with Him. I believe I was led by the Holy Spirit, as peace came over me all of a sudden. After I prayed, I felt complete peace and somehow knew that God was working on my eyesight. I was going to make my way into the city centre to meet my mom and also to purchase my lenses. The supported accommodation is a non-smoking environment, so if you want to smoke, you have to go into the back yard. I decided to go out into the yard for a fag before leaving the house to meet my mom. As I walked out into the yard, one of the other residents was smoking. As I lit my cigarette, he said to me, "I've got something to tell you, but I don't want you to say anything to Pauline." I asked him what was it so secret that he didn't want Pauline to know. He told me he had found my glasses on the branch of a tree on the side road by the supported accommodation. I almost choked on my cigarette as I digested this piece of information. He pointed to a huge tree right next to the back yard. I didn't say much to him; I left the house after smoking and went to meet my mom. I called Pauline and told her what had happened that morning. She was praising God and told me she would be over to the house later, as she was out with her grandchildren shopping. When I saw my mom, I told her what had happened that morning, and she was puzzled. I don't think she believed that my prayer had been answered; she thought this was a coincidence. As a result of getting my glasses back, I gave the money I was going to use to purchase the lenses to my mom, as she did not have much money.

I returned to the supported accommodation a few hours later to find Pauline sitting with a couple of the residents. Amos, the man who had said he'd found my specs in a tree, was also present. Pauline asked him to go and get my glasses out of his room. When he brought the case containing my specs down to us in the living-room area, my heart skipped a beat, as I instantly recognised the case. Pauline opened the case, and there were my glasses, exactly as I had left them. Pauline and I asked Amos to be totally honest and tell us where he had got the glasses, how long he claimed to have had them, and why he had decided to admit to having them in his possession. He said he had seen the glasses case in the tree about four days before. He then took them off the branch and took them to his room, as he wanted to give them to one of his daughters, but when he saw me trying to read books and paperwork, he said he couldn't do it and so decided to let me know that he had them in his room. I believed him simply because it had been five weeks since I'd thrown my stuff out with the glasses, and if he'd taken them out of the bag then, he would have given them to his daughter or, he'd have given them back to me a week after I got rid of them, as I recalled that he was one of the residents who did not agree with me throwing my optical wear away. Even my mom and Pauline thought I'd gone too far with getting rid of those lenses and the glasses. Pauline took the case and went into the spirit realm. When she opened her eyes, she confirmed that Amos was telling the truth and that my glasses had been placed on the branch by an Angel. However, she said the Angel was from the forces of darkness; this wasn't an angelic Angel. She said not to worry and that we needed to destroy the glasses, because she said that Jesus had told her that if I had placed the glasses on my eyes without seeking the Lord through prayer, then I would have been back on drugs before the end of that night. I believed her, as the taste of crack cocaine had returned to my mouth for a split second in the morning, but I had just disregarded it. Also, the day before, I had had a big argument with Elaine about the correct way to smoke crack cocaine. I found myself defending the drug and getting quite angry with her, as I was a master at crack and felt that she was trying to tell me otherwise. Pauline stood in the midst of this commotion but didn't open her mouth to say a word to me or Elaine. However, she did tell me that she thought I should go and apologise to Elaine after the argument. I went to Elaine's room and said I was sorry, and I recall thinking to myself, "What was all of that about?" I also couldn't understand why I had felt the need to defend a drug which was no longer in my life. I also found it a bit weird that I had resisted the urge to take the glasses from Amos when he told me that he had them in his room. Pauline said a prayer over the glasses and sanctified them with praying the blood of Jesus Christ. After she did that, I was able to put the glasses on, and my eyesight was restored. I was just so happy to have my eyesight back and I thanked God.

Over the next few weeks, I carried on as normal doing my job. I'd had a few dealings with the police, the probation service, charity service providers, and the prison service regarding referrals. Whenever any of the authorities called, they asked to speak to me. I also had information regarding any referrals faxed to me regularly. As this was a rehabilitation project for people with problems, the aim was to rehabilitate the homeless, people who had been released from prison, people with alcohol dependency, substance misuse and people who had support needs learning life skills.

One of the service providers referred a man who was named Mark. We started dating and ended up having a relationship. We slept together a couple of times, and I clearly recall not being able to pray to God after the first time we'd slept together although it did feel right sleeping with him at the time., I told Pauline that I was in a relationship with Mark, and she was not happy with the situation. She told me that it was not God's will for me to be with someone in the dark. She told me to go and seek God. I feel I have to stress that she didn't judge me or make me feel like I had sinned. What she did do was guide me back to God. I went before the Lord and prayed and I recall saying to God, "I'm not sorry for what I have done, because I haven't done anything wrong, but there is a reason why I couldn't pray to you, so forgive me, Father, and show me the error of my ways. Show me my secret faults." I also didn't believe that the God I served was going to be discriminating, so I began to plead my case about the relationship I was in. Little did I realise that I had an idol in my eye when I took Mark to God in prayer. I truly didn't know what to say sorry for. I hadn't committed adultery, and my knowledge of God was very limited at that time. I now understand why Pauline was not happy with the situation I had found myself in. Sometimes, people who are looking at a relationship without any emotional attachment may be able to see the bigger picture and I believed that Pauline had done that. God rebuked me by taking me out a couple of days after I sinned. Let me take you on this awesome journey. I was getting ready to worship, and I felt the grip of God on my person; His presence was very strong. I immediately sat on my bed and waited for Him to speak. The Holy Spirit told me to shower quickly and get dressed. He even told me what to wear. I did what I was instructed. When I was dressed, I was fiddling about in my room, and the stern voice of God came to me, telling me to drop what I was doing and leave my room. It catapulted me out of the door. I was trembling and trying to move as fast as I could. I went out of the front door and onto the road, and He directed my steps by telling me to turn left or right. By now I knew that God was taking me to Haven Dale Park, which was about a ten-minute walk from the supported accommodation. I was directed to go a different way. If I walked too quickly, the gentle voice said, "Slow down, child." When I got to the park, the most eye-opening, amazing thing happened to me and my surroundings. The Holy Spirit led me around the lake where there were ducks and swans. As I looked at my surroundings, God showed me things in great detail. The water that normally looked dirty was clean, clear, and beautiful. Although I do think that the ducks and swans are lovely creatures, they looked absolutely beautiful, and they had God's glory upon them. As I walked along the path, God pointed out little things that I had never noticed before. Although the path was primarily for pedestrians, vehicles did use the path at a 5-m.p.h. speed limit. I heard a car behind me, and as I was about to look back, God spoke, telling me not to look back. I looked back, thinking that it was my inner voice. I was told again, "Do not look back," and the voice was stern, unlike the first time I heard it. I spoke to God and said, "I looked back because I heard a car behind me and didn't want to get run over by it." He answered me by telling me to trust in Him and not to look back but to have faith in Him and keep on walking and listening to His voice. As I continued to walk, God showed me two men and a dog. I asked Him, "Why are you showing me this, Lord?" He replied, "The man with the dog is selling the other man drugs." When I looked properly, I could see myself scoring off a dealer. I could also see myself selling drugs to a drug user! God then spoke again and said, "So now that you can see what I wanted you to see, do you want to go back to that life?" I shook my head and said, "No, God, I do not." He didn't reply to that. He told me to keep walking, so I did. As I got to the other side of the park, everything I looked at had God's glory and was beautiful. Even the rubbish on the floor and in the dust bins that were overflow were beautiful; the weeds looked like beautiful flowers on a glorious day. The dust on the ground was not dirty; the houses opposite the park were immaculate in appearance. I was then led towards a man on a park bench with a couple of bags on the ground, and his head was buried in his hands. God said to me, "Take a good look." Although it was a man on the bench, I immediately saw myself when I was on drugs, homeless, and stealing to fund my drug habits. I felt so sad for this stranger that I recall wanting to put my arms around him and tell him everything would be all right, but I refrained myself from doing so. As I walked away and blinked, everything looked ugly and tainted, the way I'd seen the park in the past. The glory of God was snatched from my sight in a split second. Although I knew that God was still with me, His presence eased up, and I instantly knew that God was showing me that without Him, I was nothing. I discovered later on that day that the power of God is powerful. It sobered me up somewhat as the realisation began to sink that I could easily have been like the people I had seen in the park if not for God's power upon my life. I returned home after my walk, and I was beginning to know the fear of the Lord is the beginning of wisdom.

Whilst in prayer to God, I asked Him to show me a sign regarding Mark. What I still didn't realise was that I was going to God with Mark in my thoughts. I was willing God's words to me to be ones I wanted to hear. I also said to God, "Every time I have prayed to You, Lord, You have shown me something really nice about him." I did not realise that I was blinded by my desire. God even showed me in dreams what Mark was really like, but I truly believed it was my mind or the devil trying to play tricks on me. I'd seen that Mark was not a nice person and was full of lies and deceit. A stranger told me in my dreams that he was a two-timer and wasn't really interested in me but thought I looked good on his arm to impress his cronies. I continued to have a relationship with Mark, as I believed that I was doing nothing wrong, and that God had shown me the nice things about Mark. After we slept together again, I started praying to God with my mouth and not with my heart. When God clearly spoke to me that day, His words were very clear: "I command you not to sleep with him again!" I was mortified! I began to argue with God, saying, "How can you say that to me, God? I'm in a relationship with him; it feels right. He is my heart's desire, and what could possibly happen if I sleep with him again?" God didn't answer me. A vision flashed before my eyes that I couldn't ignore. I saw myself lying on my bed with a lot of blood between my legs. I wanted to believe that it was a trick of the devil again. I also wanted to believe that it wasn't God's voice that I had heard; deep down in the pit of my gut, I knew it was the voice of God.

For the next three weeks we continued dating, but every time we were alone, Mark grew tired and fell asleep. I knew this was the work of God (Mark's intuition) because when He told me not to sleep with Mark again, I told God that the relationship between Mark and me was intense and that as we'd already slept together it was likely to happen again. I also said to God in prayer that if He commanded that I do not sleep with

Mark again, then God would have to please do the work for me, as I was weak and I believed that we were doing the most natural thing on earth as man and woman. My period was late that month, so I took a pregnancy test and discovered I was pregnant. Mark and I sat and talked about it, and I decided I was keeping my child with or without him. So that was it—I was having a baby! I was so sure that God's commandment was only for a while, as I was bringing a new-born baby into the world. When I say I thought it was only for a while, I mean that I truly thought that the commandment only stood for a few weeks. Now that I was officially having a baby, God would forgive me if I slept with Mark again, because I was now pregnant and sleeping with him wasn't going to alter the fact that I was now an expectant mother. We slept with each other Thursday night, the day after I did the test, as I believed the damage or deed had been done. In the past, it had felt normal and natural, but on this night, I came face-to-face with the devil of old. Mark spoke and acted in exactly the same way as my ex-partner Darren, and my eyes were finally opened. God had shown me signs in my dreams that this man was not what I wanted him to be, and I had ignored the dreams even as I knew in my heart that he was all the things that God had shown me. After that night of lust, that final time, I surrendered and asked God to show me the man I believed to be the one for me, and I asked God not to hold back to spare me any humiliation. God didn't hesitate in showing me what sort of person Mark really was. It is my prayer that God the Father has mercy on Mark's soul. I also pray that God has mercy on my soul, as I didn't take heed and disobeyed the voice of God.

It was a Saturday morning when I woke up and saw the pool of blood between my legs. I was shocked even though God had shown me what would happen if I slept with Mark again. I hurt so much and couldn't bear the fact that my disobedience had cost me a life!

A couple of weeks after the miscarriage, I left the supported accommodation, as I didn't want to be in the house with bad memories. I no longer worked there, I'd split-up with Mark, and I'd lost my baby. I'd lost my job, as Killway Services had been informed by another resident (who was a mate of Mark's) about our relationship. It wasn't only the relationship that lost me the job. One of the Killway employees had given Pauline the impression that she was disgusted that Pauline could have an ex-offender with a string of convictions longer than most clients she had dealt with working in a place where other ex-convicts resided. Pauline had made it quite clear to me that Alice didn't like the fact that I had moved on with my life and the credit was not going to Killway Services, as they were the support team who had referred me to the supported accommodation from my last prison sentence. I wasn't too bothered by what was said, however, it seems that when you move on with your life in a positive way, certain people don't accept the drastic change. That statement is not a fact; however, it is my personal opinion, and I am entitled to voice my opinion. I felt cheated. I felt that the world owed me too much. I was hurting inside, and I wanted to continue to hurt, as it seemed normal to hurt after what had happened during those few weeks. God's unfailing power, removed the hurt. He showed up and showed off yet again in my life and snatched all the hurt and pain from me. I returned to my parents' home in Stechford. Although I still prayed and worshipped God and was still hearing from God and still poured my heart out to Him, something was missing from my life. I initially thought that once I was no longer in the supported accommodation, it was going to be hard to keep this relationship with God, but I repented before the Lord and was a lot more diligent in seeking Him. I was alone in my room a lot of the time. The fact that I repented helped. I was also led by faith to fast for twenty-one days, which I believe made me weak so that God could reveal Himself to be strong in me. The Holy Spirit continued to minister to me, comfort me, provide for me, and wrap His spiritual arms around me, and His angels had complete charge over me. I did slip a couple of times by having a bottle of wine here and there. I could drink two or three glasses of wine or sherry, but then I found that I couldn't look up to God to pray earnestly. The grace of God was upon me, and I quickly remembered that I was now a child of God. I had to pick myself up and repent every time I did wrong in the sight of the Lord. I felt God's presence come down on me, and His presence was so acute He couldn't be ignored.

CHAPTER 12

REUNITED WITH JESUS CHRIST

I went to a Methodist Church with my mom so that I could receive the word from God, but all I received was a banging headache. Please don't get me wrong; the minister was a lovely lady and extremely welcoming, as was the huge congregation. There were black people, white people, old people, young people—all types of different people, but the service itself I felt was very empty. If anything, I came out of the church and was in a horrible mood, a mood I hadn't felt for a long time. I had to take this one to God in prayer. He told me to contact Pauline, but I tried to protest, as I felt that I didn't want to run to her with every problem I had when it came to learning to walk a life with Christ. In the end, I surrendered to Him and obeyed His command. I am glad that I obeyed Him, because when I called her, it was as if we had never been apart. She asked how I was doing, and I told her about the church I attended with my mom, and she immediately said to me, "Why don't you come back?" I didn't hesitate and was back in the church that Pauline and her husband ran that Sunday. The congregation was less than a quarter as large as the congregation at my mom's church, but the word of God that was being preached was strong, and I left full of positivity. I came out of church with such a spring in my step that I'm sure I bounced all the way back home!

What I would like to stress is that my opinion and the opinion of fellow Christians is that Christianity is not a religion. Christianity is simply having a relationship with Jesus Christ (Gods word in the Bible) through the Holy Spirit (Our clear intuitive voice within). The relationship is granted to us by the Grace of God.

As I was still living at my parents' home, I wanted my own independence. I contacted the housing department and was told that I had points to bid for a home, as I had been on the waiting list since February 2011. I was getting quite frustrated with the wait and the way I felt that society treated me because I had a criminal record, so I ran to God and asked Him what was happening with my accommodation. Because I needed to know, I sought Him diligently, as I wanted to be where God told me to be. When He spoke and said that I would be moving back to the same are where Pauline's supported accommodation was, I have to admit that it wasn't the answer I wanted. I felt as though I was moving backwards in life. I tried to fight it and gave God lots of excuses and promises that if I could stay at my mom's, I would still worship Him and still attend church. I have come to realise that sometimes when we're trying to please God and ourselves, we can get it very wrong. Trusting in God is a must if we're to live a fulfilling, and abundant life of faith. When God has a plan for you, He will find a way of conveying His message to you. After all, He is the author and finisher of our faith. I can now see through the grace of God that moving back to the supported accommodation was the work of God. After God told me to move back to the same area where I had previously lived in the supported accommodation, I asked Him to show me a sign why I should move back to the supported accommodation. Some of my family members openly attacked me, saying that I was taking this Christianity too far, and there was a time when my mom questioned me regarding the Bible, but this wasn't enough for me to want to get up and leave. One Sunday, I was at Church when Pauline's husband who was the Pastor was preaching and said; "when we are given a word from God, but we are not sure what it means, we may ask for God to give us a sign He preached Mark 16:17, and these sins will follow those who believe, He then concluded his message with signs will follow us" not us following signs. I sought God again about moving just to be sure that it was God I had heard from in my intuition and not my psychological mind because the devil speaks to us too through the mind, and I really wanted to be sure that it was God who had spoken to me. The spirit in me moved me, and I instantly knew it was God; however, for selfish reasons, I didn't like the fact that I was to move back to the supported accommodation, but I was not about to disobey God again. You may ask, "How do you know it was God and not your human inner voice? How can you be certain?" The answer is that I can tell by how I feel when I'm about to do something after seeking God. If I feel discomfort, then it's not of God. If I feel peace and boldness, it's of God. You cannot ignore the feeling of peace if you seek God with diligence and an open heart. I also speak in tongues a lot, and that helps build up my spirit and enables me to keep in line with God and His will for me. It also enables me to receive from God, as it subjects my soul to the workings of the Holy Spirit. I am now back here at the supported accommodation, and one of the reasons was to write this book. Although I started to put pen to paper in August this year (2011), whilst living at Mom's, it has been much easier for me to sit down and do this here. There were far too many distractions when I lived at my mom's, and I am a person who needs to be focused on what I'm doing, as I've been easily distracted in the past. It is also a fact that the presence of God in this supported accommodation cannot be ignored. Being back here has been a wake-up call, as I forgot a lot of the things I have been through. It's strange not to think of drugs and to forget sometimes that I actually lived that life.

Whilst I was living at my mom's, I saw a lot of things that opened my eyes. For the first few weeks, I did not see any drug users and dealers. I walked down the road without seeing a single soul who was from my past life. I walked past phone boxes where there was almost always someone scoring or waiting for a dealer, but I did not see that at all. I could hear the voice of my intuition as I walked down some familiar roads and I felt as though I was being guided. Then one day I saw three drug dealers in the space of ten minutes. One dealer, who was dealing to a couple of users, didn't recognise me at first, but when he recognised me, he didn't know what to say to me. I could tell that he was embarrassed for selling drugs to me in the past, and I felt great compassion for him. The dealer said that he didn't believe in God and congratulated me for turning my life around. I explained to him that I did not do anything and that I just woke up one day and the drugs lifestyle had disappeared. He couldn't understand that I was telling him that the work he saw in me was not of my doing. It was God who delivered me. I knew he didn't understand as I didn't really understand how the transformation had happened to me either. After speaking to the dealer, I said my good-byes and began walking down the road towards my aunt's house. I heard a car pull up beside me, and there were two other drug dealers looking at me with puzzled expressions on their faces. One dealer said, "I'd heard that you were around, but I didn't believe that you were clean." Now that he had seen me with his own eyes, he was very subdued. Again, I told him about my experience that how I was delivered from darkness over night, and I told him that I believed it was God and to my surprise, he was in total agreement. He too looked ashamed that he had sold me drugs in the past. The biggest shock came a couple of weeks later when I saw a dealer who was called Mr Big. He was big in body and in reputation. We were both in a corner shop waiting to be served. I spoke to the sales assistant. He didn't recognise me until he heard my voice. He almost collapsed in the shop! He kept on justifying himself to me by saying that he had never really wanted to sell me drugs and that he had always known I was better than other smokers. I recall thinking, "That's a lie; I was no better than my drug pals. If anything, I was worse, and you know it!" He kept saying that I had a guardian angel, and I noticed that whenever he said this, he looked above my head and around my body as if he could see something. This didn't unnerve me, quite the opposite. He couldn't understand how someone could wake up one day and have the past thirteen years removed. I kind of know where he was coming from as I could not get my head around it too. I haven't forgotten where I came from. I have all the knowledge of living in the dark, but I feel as though I am talking about somebody who I once knew very well, and it feels like the old me is now dead and a new woman has entered my body.

One day, I had an urge to contact Pauline to ask her how she was. Pauline and I had fallen out before I left but something told me to contact her. Pauline sounded very surprised to hear my voice and she said that she thought I had gone back on drugs or was in prison. I reassured her that I was OK and that I was living with my parents. I mentioned that I was missing the church that she attended and she said to me, "why don't you come back to the church?" I agreed and was in church the following Sunday. It was lovely seeing the old familiar faces and I recall the church service being powerful. I attended church every Sunday and after a few weeks, Pauline offered me a room to move in as a volunteer live in staff. I decided to move back to Pauline's supported accommodation. I was back in room 1 and I quickly adjusted to living in the supported accommodation helping as a volunteer.

Since coming back to the supported accommodation and returning to the church, I have been baptised in water; I was baptised with the Holy Spirit in March 2011, and this is when I received the grace to speak in tongues, and then I had a water baptism in July 2011. I have received the gifts of speaking in tongues, the interpretation of tongues, prophecy, discerning of the spirits, and many more gifts that God has blessed me with, distributing them to me as He wills (1 Corinthians 12:4-11). Some of my family members were a little bit sceptical; they believed it was too soon to be baptised, because I'd only been a Christian for a few months. Because of the life I had before finding Christ, I needed to be sure that I knew what I was doing. I achieved that by reading the Bible stories about baptism and learning why people were baptised. In my opinion I believe that one has to believe with their heart. God loves us, but hates sin, and He came to the earth so that we may have and enjoy life and have it till it overflows (John 10:10). He preaches the gospel and turns us to change our way of thinking also known as repentance (Luke 15:7). I still pinch myself as it is a wonderful feeling to be free from the dark path I once walked. Life is full of challenges but having an inner guide makes it so much easier when we are faced by the challenges. For me I see life without Christ is a crisis. Walking in the light is not just about attending church and reading the Bible; it's about getting to know Jesus and abiding in Him (John15:1–12). Now I have truly seen the light, and I'm guided to walk in the light. I know that no matter what anyone thinks of me, no matter what judgements are made about me and my life (because I know I will be judged), no matter what is put in my path as I walk through life, I finally have reached my resting place on this earth. If God is for me, who can be against me? I have a solid promise from the God I serve: "I will make your paths straight" (Hebrews 12:13). I rest in the comfort of God, Jesus Christ of Nazareth. Amen.

A FINAL WORD ON BOOK 1

A Change of Lifestyle Is Very Necessary

Before I take you into Book 2 of Trapped by The Devil, I just want to share my take on what it means for me to live as a Christian. To me, a Christian way of life is a personal experience. According to the Bible, us Christian's are to renew our minds daily by the Word of God. We have 2 important parts to our mind. The conscious mind and the subconscious part of the mind. (I discuss this a little later in Book 2). In a nutshell, our conscious mind is ONLY creative and our subconscious mind is where we have a mental program that controls 96-98% of our life. By renewing the mind daily, we are able to change the mental program from a negative program into a positive program. This practice takes the desire to want to change and the persistence to continue. Having God in our life (hearing and knowing our intuition) helps us to persist with faith that all things work together for our good.

This Is for My Family

Losing contact with my family was due to the prison life I chose to live. I'm not saying that I directly went out of my way to go to jail, but I cannot ignore the fact that I made a single decision and it led me down a path of darkness as I was a criminal twenty-four hours a day, and going to jail was part of the lifestyle. Having a close relationship with my family is very important to me, as I've lost so many years. I cannot turn the clock back but I can determine that I will remain in my faith, which will help me to be the best version of me for my loved ones.

To Friends and Acquaintances

I shared with you my journey of my true life story and the way I lived. I have learned to forgive and forget the wrongs that people have done to me over the years, as that was the only way that I could find real peace in my heart. I've also been an enemy to people over the years, and for your sake, I hope you find it in your hearts to forgive me. When we forgive other's for their wrong doings, we are freeing ourselves and so forgiveness is a way of dropping any heavy burdens, and what I did to hurt you is really not worth you having any sleepless nights. Have I forgiven the man whom I lived a life of hell with? Yes I have and I was only able to do so as I now understand that forgiveness is for me and not for him or anyone else. Carrying hate, fear and pain only hurts me, the pain I carried can not hurt anyone but myself. I also understand that forgiveness is a process but the more we understand what it means to forgive, the more we understand why we could do it. There are no 'shoulds' or 'must', its more of we could if we would.

To Readers of This Book

I want you to know that it was hard to recount the dreadful times of my journey, but it's not about me; it's about sharing what I went through to help others who may feel overwhelmed with their current or past situation and may need a bit of inspiration to help them out.

I currently run a 4 month mentorship program called 3-steps-2-freedom where I help and support clients who want to work on their personal growth to have, be and do what they truly desire.

For more information, please send an email to info@redflagwellbeing. co.uk

God bless you all x

A note from the Author

I have come to realise that personal development has helped me on my journey. The Bible mentions the heart of man and

how important it is for believer's to be diligent to have the word of God in our hearts.

Just for this explanation, let's replace the word God, Father, and The Holy Spirit with the word intuition and eternal life.

Our intuition is one of our higher faculties and is the voice of God (also called the Holy Spirit). Eternal life is what we have as life never really ends

If you want to know how, please feel free to contact by sending an email to info@redflagwellbeing.co.uk

Kate – Life journey and how to contact Kate.

Trapped by the Devil is the astonishing story of Kate was set free from a life of mental health problems, domestic abuse, crime and drug addiction. The power of God dramatically transformed this woman whose life seemed to be irreversibly spiralling out of control.

Since writing the book in 2011, the Author has gone on to help drug addicts overcome drug addiction with profound results, she has achieved a licence to teach Zumba Fitness since February 2012, a diploma in understanding mental health at a Level 3, The Author is also a qualified Personal Trainer and class instructor, a nutritionist, a specialist at delivering her unique and powerful mentorship programme called 3-steps-2-freedom that fine tunes the soul to allow our great human potential to flourish, grow and create from using our authority and power and, The Author is the CEO and founder of her Not-for-profit company which is an organisation that offers care & support to some of the most vulnerable adults who have complex support needs and mental health illness. The Author's company bridges the gap between regulated care services and registered social landlords in the UK. The Author is also a consultant and mentor.

In the Author's words, "I am honoured to share my true life story with the readers of this book. I hope broken hearts are healed and I hope I have shone a light in to the life of a lost and broken souls".

BOOK 2 OF TRAPPED BY THE DEVIL

VISUALISATION TO FREEDOM

After writing my first book in 2012, my life was very exciting. I was seeing one miracle after another and I was in a state of bliss. I found it hard to accept that my life could do a 360 degree turn with no explanation, so I decided to investigate how it all happened.

When I arrived at the supported accommodation back in 2011, I was very fortunate to fall into the arms of a mentor. This lady helped me to understand some fundamental truths about life. My mentor explained the science of thinking and used a drawing of a stick person to illustrate the lessons. I fell in love with this concept as I could relate to the stick person presentation as it helped me to understand the 2 parts of the mind, the conscious mind and the subconscious mind. I was able to see how I came out of a life of destruction at the blink of an eye. Here is what I discovered whilst studying the science of thinking.

There maybe a number of aspects to the human mind. I want to talk about 2 parts of the mind. The conscious mind and the subconscious mind.

The conscious mind: This part of our mind is the intellect mind. We are aware of our environment and we are able to use this part of our mind to think. Thinking is a conscious skill and does not constitute for mental activity. If we are to think, we will use our higher faculties to create the life we desire. Our higher faculties are;

- Perception
- Reason
- Will
- Imagination
- Intuition
- Memory

As I mentioned in book one, I used the imagination quite often to dream of a life of bliss and happiness when I was caught up in the drugs world. At the time, I did not know that I was tapping into one of the higher faculties as I thought I was just escaping my current reality. I decided to take this journey of personal development seriously as I quickly realised that life experiences are not a coincidence nor is life accidental. I also learned that life is governed by universal laws and our attitude towards the universal laws will determine what quality of life we experience. We as humans have 2 choices... life or death? In other words, victim of circumstances or victory over challenges. I chose life and victory.

I am not going to delude myself or the readers of this book by saying that life is easy, life is challenging, but we can win if we know and understand the rules of life. Let's look at life as a game. Games have rules. If we understand and stick to the rules, we win. If we are ignorant of the rules then we automatically violate the universal laws and we eventually loose. This fundamental truth can be seen throughout the ages.

CHAPTER 1

HOW IT ALL BEGAN FOR ME

My life is bliss, I am learning so much about Christianity and the universal laws. I would not say I felt a sense of loneliness, but I did desire to meet a partner who I would love and who would love me in return. I decided to pray about this. My prayer was very simple and straight to the point. I recall asking God if I was to meet my perfect match. After I asked, I waited for my intuition to speak. The answer was yes! That was it! I asked, and I received the answer. I trusted my intuition and so I would imagine the feeling of being loved by a man. As I mentioned in the first book, I had never really found love nor had I loved anyone apart from my family. I told my mentor about my desire and my mentor told me that I would meet my soulmate and that we would be a very successful couple. I continued to visualise being happy with my perfect partner every morning and during the day, I continued working as a volunteer doing support worker duties at the supported accommodation.

In September 2011, there was a knock at the door of the supported accommodation. I answered the door and before me stood 2 civil servants. One was male and the other was female. They both smiled and the male officer asked me if Elaine was in. I said "yes" and before I knew it, both officers were inside the supported accommodation. The female officer stayed by the front door, and the male officer walked passed me and headed for the conference room where Elaine was sat with Pauline. After a couple of minutes, the male officer came out of the conference room and he and the female civil servant both left. I later spoke with Elaine and she said that the male officer was a nice person who just popped in to check her well-being as she had reported an incident to the police earlier in the year and this was a follow up visit. On Friday 13th January 2012, the male civil servant returned to the supported accommodation but this time he was accompanied by 2 other male officers. I answered the front door and the officer asked for Elaine. Elaine was in her room which was upstairs so I asked the officers to give me a minute to let Elaine know that they were asking to see her. Elaine came downstairs and saw the officers. The 3 officers sat in the communal living room and engaged in conversation with Elaine, the service users and myself. We spoke about nothing in particular. The officer who visited Elaine last year September was friendly and had lovely warm eyes. He was also a bit of a comedian and made us laugh with his jokes. The 3 officers remained in the supported accommodation for a while. I felt as though one officer was drawn to me and me to him. I then began to think of how lovely it would be to meet my Mr. Right. Whilst in the supported accommodation, the officers had an emergency call come over their radio and all 3 got up to leave. As they were leaving, one officer scribbled down his mobile contact number on a piece of cardboard and handed it to me. As he passed it to me I noticed he had put his first name on the card. His name was Mike. Mike looked me in my eyes and said "Call me when you are free". I took the piece of cardboard off him, smiled and I put it in my pocket. I kept thinking to myself that this is weird. I liked him a lot but I could not see us in a serious relationship due to his career and my past encounters with the law.

CHAPTER 2

JUDGED FOR FALLING IN LOVE

I went to church on Sunday15ᵗʰ January and when I returned, I decided to call the officer. I recall my palms being sweaty and I was a bit nervous. After a short while, I picked up my phone to call him. Mike answered the phone. We said our hello's and I recall feeling a bit awkward and at one point I wished I had not called him. During our telephone conversation I kept thinking "What if he asks any questions about what I had done previous to working at the supported accommodation?" Mike did not ask me any awkward questions and was very person centred and was more focused on my well-being and telling me how much he liked me. Mike told me that he would love to see me again. He told me that as he worked in the area, he was always in the near to the supported accommodation and said he could pop in to see me when he had a few minutes or we could go for a coffee when he was free. We began seeing each other as well as texting and calling each other daily. Mike was always mindful that I was at work and sometimes we would meet down the road from the supported accommodation. We had a wonderful friendship. Mike would always kiss me on my cheek or a gentle kiss on the lips. This is when I realised that he was a true gentleman. I really liked him but I would dread the day I told him about my past. I was certain that he would run a mile.

In February of 2012, my mentor decided to pay for me and her daughter Joanne, to go to Liverpool for the day to train to become Zumba Fitness

Instructors. We both travelled down to Liverpool on the train, took the Zumba Instructor masterclass and we both received our license to teach Zumba Fitness classes. This helped my confidence as I had always loved dancing and I was given a second chance to live out my dream. Joanne helped me with finding a hall and she also advised me on how to work with clients. I listened to her advice and started my very first class in a church hall not too far from Pauline's supported accommodation. As I was still in receipt of benefits, I made the Job Centre aware of the change in my circumstances and they helped me with becoming self employed. I recall feeling empowered as I never believed that I would be doing something I loved as a career. Being addicted to drugs and living a life as a criminal had really damaged my self-image and my mentor was showing me how to overcome barriers and feel empowered. One day in May of 2012, my mentor called me to ask me if I would like a car. I was speechless and graciously accepted her offer. My mentor offered me her husbands car as he had recently brought another car. We took the car to a local garage to have it checked over, but one of the mechanics advised that I should drive a smaller car. My mentor part exchanged her husbands old car for a little blue Peugeot 103. I immediately fell in love with my new car. In just over one year, my life had changed dramatically and I was always thanking God. Mike was always very supportive of my new career and was always telling me that I am amazing and that I deserved all the good things in life. After a few months of us dating each other, I decided to tell Mike about my past. I was so nervous and prepared myself for the worse. Mike was very busy with work and I did not want to tell him about my past over the phone or via text message but every time we arranged to meet, he would cancel on the day, or he would have to work. I was getting frustrated as I wanted to let him know that I had a colourful past. This was very important to me as I was falling in love with him and I felt that he should know my past due to the nature of his career. Whilst I was seeing Mike, I attracted the media with my story and I appeared in the local newspaper. The Job Centre had reported my success story and so I was interviewed by newspaper reporters. I had been waiting for the right moment to talk to Mike about my past for weeks but he was always too busy and so our conversations were mainly on the phone. When my story appeared in the local paper, it was nice to see how far I had come in such a short space of time but because I had not told Mike about my past, he would learn about me from a newspaper. The article was a positive story but I still felt that Mike should hear it from me. The day after the story had gone out I saw Mike. He looked happy to see me and I had a glimmer of hope about our relationship. I told him about the article in the papers. Mike was not moved by my story. He said that he has been a civil servant officer for almost 30 years and so he had an idea that I was once in a dark place but he said that he could see that I was no longer that person who led that life. He went on to say that everyone has a past and we have all done things we would rather forget. He also said that he could see that I was a lovely caring person and to him, that is the most important quality. I could not believe how genuine, lovely and special Mike was! He also said that he is happy for us to take as long as possible getting to know each other before we decide to have an intimate relationship. Mike said that I was very precious to him and that he did not want to rush anything between us. He reassured me that he was not going anywhere and that he was drawn to me mainly due to my love for Jesus as he was a Catholic man. He said that he could see that I was genuine with my Christian walk and he felt the tug on his heartstrings every time he thought of me. My life had become quite busy as I was finding my feet again. Pauline encouraged me to create a social media account with Facebook. I was nervous to begin with but I soon connected with some familiar faces of people I knew. I often scrolled Facebook looking for some old school friends. I recall finding some friends and viewing their profile pictures but I did not have the confidence to connect with them as I did not want to answer any awkward questions on my past. The day that my story appeared in the newspaper, I recall having over 40 new friend requests from old school friends and other people I knew from my past before my drug life. I embraced them all. People where really nice to me and were telling me how strong I was to have come out of the challenges of a life of drugs, abuse and crime. They were also inspired by the newspaper article and they commended me for being so brave for coming out of the challenges I faced over the years of drug abuse and addiction. I connected with some of my dearest school friends and we arranged to meet up and go for a drink in the city centre. It was a great evening and it was lovely to see them all. I also went out with my older brother on his birthday. We had a brilliant night and I recall getting back home in the early hours of Sunday morning. I did not see much of my older brother but we communicated over the telephone once or twice a month.

One day in the supported accommodation, one of the service users mentioned to Pauline that I was dating Mike and that he is a civil servant officer. Pauline was not happy with this. She arranged a meeting with her husband and myself to discuss why she felt it was not a good idea for me to be dating a police officer. We all sat in the conference room to have this meeting. I felt like a naughty child as this was not necessary, in fact, this was none of her business. Pauline said that I was breaking one of God's Holy commandments by committing adultery and that the supported accommodation was built on Holy ground and what Mike and I am doing is not right. She said that we were having sex on the premises and it must stop immediately. Pauline went on to say that a man who has worked as a police officer for any length of time would not have any real interest in someone who was once a drug addict and criminal. She continued talking by saying that Mike must have an ulterior motive to be dating me. She said that he was a married man with 3 children and she said that she knew this as she was friends with his Chief Inspector. I could not believe what she was saying. I recall telling her that Mike is not a married man but she insisted that she knew a chief Inspector and this Chief Inspector told her that Mike was married and had 3 children. Something in me knew that she was not telling the truth. Pauline also accused me of sleeping with Mike! This was outrageous!!! Mike and I had barley kissed each other. I was outraged and I said to her and her husband that I am an adult, I'm over the age of consent and Mike and I have not had sex, but if we had then it was none of her business. I felt as though she had crossed the line. Pauline and her husband dismissed what I had said. Pauline then instructed her husband to ban me from the pulpit in the church until their further investigation. I remained calm and I recall saying to both of them that no one can stop me from worshipping God and that I do not need a pulpit, I can worship God anywhere. I'm not too sure if I infuriated Pauline, because she did not stop there, she ordered me to ask Mike for his email address as she said that she will be contacting him and that he was taking advantage of a vulnerable female. I protested to what she had said about Mike. He was lovely, genuine and he was not taking advantage of me in any shape or form. Mike had plenty of opportunities for us to book a hotel for the night as we were not breaking the law! I was so upset after the meeting for a number of reasons. I understood that Pauline could be a little bit suspicious of Mike showing interest in a woman who's past was so unstable, I get it, but she had absolutely no right in accusing us of having sex on the premises, she had no right in calling a meeting with her husband to discuss my personal life and I had a gut feeling that she was lying through her teeth about being friends with Mike's Chief Inspector. I contacted Mike to tell him what had happened. Mike said he was confused and vehemently denied ever being married and he said he does not have any children. He also asked what is Pauline's issue with me dating a decent man? Mike said he could understand that Pauline may be protective over me as she had nurtured me and became my mentor, but he said that still does not give her the right to behave in this manner. Mike gave me his email address as he said he had nothing to hide but he could not believe what Pauline had said and done. Pauline said that she will contact Mike's Sergeant within a few days but she never did. I guess it was because there was nothing to report and I think she did some reflecting. I understood the affection this lady had for me and I understood that she had really helped me with my personal development and I will always be very grateful, however, this did not give her the right to control who I decided to date. As I was learning to forgive others of their mistakes, it did not take me too long to move on with my life without any ill feelings towards Pauline, but we did not speak of the meeting we had that day, nor did we mention what was said in the meeting again. I continued to go to church and I sang and worshipped God as I stood with the rest of the congregation.

Around July/August of 2012, I recall really yearning to have my own accommodation. I kept using visualisation to see myself living independently in a 3 bedroom house. One day, I had to go to the High Street. I parked my car in a car park, and I made my way to the High Street. I was walking on a pavement and the next thing I recall is being shoved from behind and I fell on a lady who was also walking on the pavement. I had no idea what had happened. The lady quickly got up and began shouting at a man who was driving a huge lorry. I was in shock as I recall hearing this lady shouting at the driver to stop his vehicle as he had hit me from behind. I soon realised what had happened. The back end of the lorry had tapped me on my left shoulder and that was what had caused me to fall on this lady. The driver of the lorry got out of his vehicle and was apologising to me and the lady. The car park manager had also witnessed me being hit by the lorry. I wasn't in any pain, I was just in shock as the lorry was huge and I was finding it hard to comprehend that a vehicle of that size hadn't sent me flying over to the other side of the large car park. I recall the lady speaking on my behalf as she took the driver's details and the vehicle registration number. I kept thanking God that she was there as I believe the driver did not know that he had hit me and he would have driven off.

I went to the local hospital to get checked over. I was fine but the doctor said I had whiplash. The next day, I received a call from a company who knew that I had been in a road traffic accident. I was puzzled how they knew. The company went to work on my behalf and made an insurance claim on my behalf. I was paid just under £4,000.00 in December 2012. Due to my strong Christian faith, I obeyed the law on tithing. I tithed 10% to the church, I put money aside for a deposit on a one bed apartment and with the rest of the money, I brought my family and myself Christmas presents. I did not give up on my vision to live in a 3 bed property but I kept telling myself that I am going in the right direction. I kept on visualising living in a 3 bed property and the feeling was amazing!

On January 3rd 2013, I moved out of the supported accommodation and moved into a one bedroom studio flat. The landlord of the accommodation was very polite and just from viewing the property, I could tell that he was a person who cared about his properties and his tenants well-being. I continued to volunteer as a support worker and Pauline was still mentoring me with my personal development journey and she still held workshops with the service users. Pauline spent a lot of time mentoring me one- to-one and I continued to grow in conscious awareness. The other service users who attended the workshops said that they did not see much of a change in their personal life but I knew that if I wanted to change my results, then I had to do different things. Some of the other service users said that I was born lucky but I realised that they were looking at my results. They were not paying attention to my actions that created my results. Mike and I continued to see each other and we remained consistent with calling and texting each other every day. Mike would spend some weekends at my home with me. Our relationship continued to blossom until one day in August 2014. I was progressing with my personal development journey but I felt that our relationship was stagnated. I loved Mike but I guess I wanted more from our relationship. We never argued and there were no trust issues but I felt that we were not progressing forward. Mike never said much about his work and due to the nature of his career we did not spend much time together and although I knew he was faithful, but I felt that our relationship had become stuck with no progression and Mike seemed too laid back and complacent. Pauline's words would still ring in the back of my mind. Pauline had said that Mike was not serious about commitment with me as she still believed he had a wife and 3 children. The thought of being the other woman made me feel physically sick but I knew Pauline was making it up about Mike having a wife and children. I trusted God as it was God who I prayed to about meeting my perfect partner who would love and respect me. My faith in God is unshakable and Mike did not behave like a man who was cheating. I am not deluded to believe that some people manage to hide there true ways from their partners, and I am not deluded to believe that all men are obvious cheats, but I was not dealing with what people say or do, I was dealing with God. When we believe in God, when we pray earnestly to God, when we can hear our intuition clearly, we have perfect direction from God. God is the one who brought Mike and me together, not coincidence and not chance, and because I spoke to God about this before Mike appeared in my life, I believe God honoured my faith and brought Mike and I together. Mike is very person centred and attentive towards me. Due to my previous lifestyle, I was so used to meeting people who had ulterior motives. People who always wanted something from you rather than giving for the sake of kindness. Mike was very gentle, kind and loving. Pauline had also made her feelings clear that she did not like the idea of me and Mike dating and often said it would not last. One day, I challenged Mike about his work and the little time we were spending together lately. I was not satisfied with his response and in anger I ended the relationship with Mike and I immediately blocked his number and deleted it. I told myself that there was more to life than this. I wanted more than a safe relationship. I wanted excitement and adventure but Mike was always working. Sometimes he worked away and I wouldn't see him for weeks on end. When I looked back, I realised that I acted out of anger. And so after two weeks of me ending the relationship, I realised I had made a huge mistake. I was missing Mike. I said I wanted more but life was empty and dull without him. I had to live with my mistake and so I threw myself deeper into Christianity, personal development, support working and I continued to teach Zumba Fitness all over the West Midlands. I told Pauline that I had ended the relationship with Mike, and I recall her looking relieved. Pauline comforted me but said I had made the right decision. I, on the other hand was not so sure about the decision I made whilst in anger. Pauline told me that I would meet the right man and she still protested that Mike was not the right man for me. Pauline also helped me with mindset training and also she stepped in when I did not manage my finances well. Pauline would always borrow me money when I needed it and I always paid Pauline back what I had borrowed and I continued to be faithful with my walk with God and tithing to the church and donating money to Pauline's supported accommodation.

I continued learning to live independently and I found it easier because I had a lot of support from Pauline and also the landlord was very good and understanding. If I could not afford to pay my rent on time, I would immediately contact the landlord to offer a payment plan. The landlord who is called Mo would always accept my offer and he never once chased me for late payments. I did not give him the reason to be concerned about how I treated my tenancy and I always kept my word with payments. My mentor always told me the importance of paying my rent and bills on time and she helped me when I needed help and support. I was the only female that lived in the property and there were 3 other studio flats. I kept myself to myself and I always greeted my neighbours when we passed on the landing. The man who lived downstairs would often play his music really loud and I would always smell cannabis. The fact he smoked drugs did not bother me but the smell lingering in the building gave me reason to complain to him on more than one occasion. I was always polite when I complained to him and he said he understood but he carried on smoking cannabis and playing his loud music. There was a single man who lived opposite me who was peaceful and who did not bother anyone except for when his 2 young children visited some weekends. The children were aged around 8 and 10 years old and they would jump, shout, scream and run up and down the landing. As I was working at the supported accommodation during the day and as I held 3 Zumba Fitness sessions in the week, I was hardly home but when I was home I just wanted to relax. Apart from the noise from 2 of the 3 neighbours, I felt safe in my home.

In December 2014, Pauline brought me a silver Mercedes Benz. I was so very grateful and I could not stop thanking her for her kindness. Pauline said that she had a strong urge to buy me the car and she said that I must have manifested it with the personal development tools I had learned on my journey. It suddenly hit me that I desired a Mercedes Benz in my visualisation sessions way back in 2002 and also recently when I saw a beautiful black Mercedes Benz on the road one day, I recalled my thoughts towards wanting to own one. I loved my new car. I loved the comfort and the style however at the beginning of 2015, I noticed that when I drove the car over 50 mph, it would shudder as if it was struggling to drive at this speed. I also had some technical issues with the indicators. I loved my vehicle but I could not ignore the fact that it had done well over 100,000 miles on the clock and maybe it's time for me to invest in a new car. Another issue was that Pauline had said that she brought me the car so that I could take some of her service users' to appointments. I did not like this idea as I felt that Pauline was being controlling. How do you give someone a gift and then tell them who they can have in the car? I also found that Pauline had a poor attitude by the way she spoke to me and others. It was really nice of her to buy me a car but that does not qualify her to talk down to me. Pauline and I had disagreements on quite a few occasion but I was being mentored by her and I would persist for the sake of my dream life and I kept my mind focused on the end goal.

I decided to contact a car leasing agency. They told me that if I qualify for car finance, I could be in my new car in a matter of a few days. As I had never purchased a car in this way before, I did not know the steps. I was told by an agent that all I need to do is find a car, find a car dealership and they will do the rest. I began searching online for a new car. Although I was self employed as a Zumba Fitness Instructor, my earnings were not that great. I started looking at cars like Fords, Seat's, Vauxhall and Peugeot's but I also found it very hard to imagine not driving a Mercedes Benz. As I was weighing up my options with the prices, I felt myself getting frustrated as I could not find a car that I really liked. As I continued my search. I finally decided to go for a Seat Leon. It was a nice car but it did not get me excited. As I looked at the car and the repayment plan, my intuition spoke and said "this is not the car you asked for". I immediately felt my heart leap. The feeling of excitement, hope and happiness filled my whole body. I whispered to my intuition saying; "I can have a Mercedes Benz?" I felt peace, confidence and assurance. I found a car dealership that was selling a black Mercedes Benz. I clicked on to the car and zoomed in on the photo. This is the car I really want. I contacted the agent who told me that he just needed to do some checks and that he would get back to me. The agent contacted me back within 10 minutes. He told me that I had passed the relevant checks and that all that I needed to do was to submit some documents over to him. The whole process took around 3-4 working days. After I had submitted bank statements and other documents, the agency said they had a problem with one of my documents and that I may not be able to have the car on finance. I felt fear and disappointment grip my throat and then I remembered what my intuition had said. I was drawn to my Bible where I read the book of Isaiah Chapter 45:2 and Isaiah Chapter 54:2-5. As soon as I read the words, I felt calm, reassured and confident and I knew that I knew, that I knew that I had my dream car! 10 minutes after me reading these scriptures, the car finance had gone through smooth and I was able to collect my car the next day. Pauline was very happy to see that I was now moving forward with life and she was embracing the changes in my life and my testimonies.

CHAPTER 3

HEARTACHE

My life continued in the direction of being self-employed and personal growth. Challenges came, I overcame most of them immediately but some challenges kept re-appearing. The pain I felt since splitting up with Mike was in the background of my mind. I continued to volunteer at the supported accommodation. The training I went through was not easy and so it made me depend on my intuition more than ever. I felt that the experiences and challenges that produced spiritual growth were needed for me to fulfil my purpose. At this point in my life, I had an idea of what my purpose was. I knew deep in my soul that I would be helping vulnerable people who had complex mental health conditions and substance misuse addictions. I often found volunteering frustrating as the role of a support worker working with vulnerable adults who presented with complex support needs could be overwhelming. Some days were easy and flowed, other days would drain my energy. As I went through life I was always mindful of a Bible scripture I had meditated on in 2011, the book of Ecclesiastes, Chapter 3:1-8. If I paraphrase the scriptures, then basically, there is a season for everything under the sun, a season to sow and a season to reap, a season to be happy and a season to be sad, a season to get and a season to loose. In a nutshell, I am to embrace every moment of life and just know that it is only for a season. I understood that this was my season of growth. The Biblical scriptures do not say how long our seasons last, but one thing is for sure, everything is for a season and then the season ends. This scripture helped me when I thought that things were overwhelming and I embraced the seasons where I experienced the natural flow of life.

In May 2015, my older brother called me one day and he sounded agitated during the call. My brother who was called Jerry, was ranting on about the police taking his car off the road due to him not having any car insurance, and now he had no means of transport for him to travel to work. He was shouting down the phone as he narrated how he was spotted in the car by 2 police officers. I listened sympathetically as I always had a soft spot for my older brother. Jerry said that the police had taken his car to a police impound and that he needed to raise £250.00. He said he needed to pay £100.00 to get his car out of the impound and £150.00 to pay the first instalment for car insurance to get his car legally back on the road. My brother said that he had managed to raise £200.00 from friends, but he still needed £50.00. My brother asked if I could please lend him the money. As I was breaking even with my income and expenses, I only had just over £50.00 in my bank account, and that money was to go towards my car insurance in a few days time. I loved my brother but I found myself being annoyed with his irresponsible behaviour. I told my brother that I cannot borrow him the money as I only have just over £50.00 to my name. I disconnected the call and as I began to walk, my intuition spoke loud and clear in my core. Intuition spoke and said "give him the money and do not ask for it back nor should you expect it back". I could not ignore what I had heard my intuition say. I decided to argue with my intuition by saying "No, it's not fair. Why should I take my hard earned cash and give it to my brother who is being irresponsible? Why should I pay the price? I have my car insurance to pay for in a few days!" My intuition did not reply and instead I felt a warm tug on my heart stings. I immediately knew that what my intuition was saying was right so I called my brother and I told him that I would give him the money he needed to get his car back. My brother sounded so happy and said that one of his friends told him to have faith as God will provide. My brother was not a Christian and often said that he did not believe there was a God. He had said that he is more inclined to believe in evolution as he thought the Bible was just a book of stories that some people believed in. I transferred the money into my brother's bank account. About 2 hours later, I spoke with my brother and he sounded defeated. My brother told me to arrange a day to come and collect my £50.00 from him as he does not know how to do bank transfers and he said he was not willing to learn a new skill today. I was a bit upset at my brother's attitude towards me when he did not get what he wanted but then I quickly remembered that it was not my idea to loan him the money in the first place as it was my intuition that prompted me to do so, I had no reason to be offended by his behaviour as this was not personal.

I arranged a date and time to go to collect my money from my brother. I recall it was a Friday evening and my brother sounded happy that I would be visiting him. When I arrived, I saw Jerry and his partner sat in the living room. I sat down and engaged in conversation with them both. After a short while, my brother asked if I could drive him to the other side of the city as he wanted to buy some barbecue food from a West Indian outdoor stall. As my brother was still in a dark place, I knew he was going to buy drugs as no one I knew would travel that far for chicken and rice. I did not judge him nor did I make my assumptions known to my brother. We got in to my car and I decided to connect my iPhone to a Bluetooth speaker. I usually played Gospel songs when I drove my car but today I played some old revival reggae songs by artists Dennis Brown, Gregory Isaac, Alton Ellis and a few more. Whilst we were driving a song came on by an artist named Errol Dunkley. My brother started to sing the lyrics and dance with his arms. He asked me how did I know that this song was his favourite song. I told him that I didn't know. The song was called 'Little Way Different'. When the song ended, my brother decided to rewind the song but he ended up damaging the Bluetooth device. I was a bit upset as I always took good care of my possessions but I didn't make a fuss, I just let it go. We arrived at the destination, my brother got out of the car to go and speak to a man who was cooking barbecue jerk chicken, I stayed in the car and turned the car around as we were parked in a road that was a dead end. Once I had positioned the car to face the way out, I waited for my brother. My brother began waving his hands in my direction and was beckoning me to come out of the car. I switched off the engine and walked over to my brother. It was only then that I looked at my brother with clear eyes. He looked painfully thin, his cheeks were gaunt, he was unkempt and he looked like a lost soul. I was convinced that my brother had also brought drugs as well as some food. I can hear him in my mind as I sit and write this book as he is standing so very proud as he is telling people that I was his little sister. I recall having mixed emotions as I stood back and watched my older brother. I felt guilt because I had been miraculously healed from a life a destruction, drugs and pain, yet my brother was still trapped and I felt helpless. If I had consciously taken steps to come out of the drugs world, I would have the ability to show others how I did it but as I was sovereignly touched by the power of God, I could not teach anyone how to be completely free of drug addiction. I also felt peace when I looked at Jerry. He had been through so much in his life and was still able to smile. This was my dear brother and I loved him with unconditional love.

We made our way back to his home. When we arrived, my brother asked me to wait in the car whilst he drops off the food to his partner and he said he would bring the £50.00 out to me. My brother returned to the car with a takeaway box that contained the jerk chicken and rice and he insisted that I take the food home. Once he passed me the food, he started to search under the passenger seat as he had mislaid his mobile phone. I called his number, his phone rang but it was not ringing in the car. He asked me to please wait whilst he went indoors to look for his phone. Jerry came out of his home with no phone and he pleaded with me to take him back to where we went to get the food from. I groaned inwardly as it was over 10 miles away. I agreed to take Jerry back to the West Indian stall. As we got close to the stall, my phone began to ring. The name Jerry was displayed on my phone. My brother answered my phone. It was his partner calling him to let him know that he had left his phone at home in their flat and that she had found it on their sofa. Without a word, I turned my car around and drove my brother back to his home. My brother said that he didn't have much money but he offered me £5.00 for the petrol. My brother thanked me for borrowing him the money and for being patient with his disruptive lifestyle. I smiled and told him it was OK. My brother got out of the car and I noticed that he had dropped some heroin wrapped in tinfoil on the passengers seat. I calmly called my brother's name, he looked at me, I told him that he had dropped something in my car. My brother looked at the heroin in the foil plate, gave me an embarrassed sheepish smile and said "Sis, please pray for me." I recall feeling great sorrow for my big brother and how empty, shallow and fickle his life seemed. As I pulled off, I prayed in tongues all the way home. When I arrived home, my spirit felt disturbed so I continued to pray until my head hit the pillow that night.

I woke up, and remembered yesterdays events with visiting my brother. I lay in silence as I contemplated the meaning of life. How could one addict be snatched from a lifestyle in the blink of an eye and yet, others may stay there until they die. I was still feeling as though something was not quite right. I got up to make a coffee and use the bathroom. The studio flat I lived in had 2 doors. The main room where my bed, TV and furniture was and another door which led to the small kitchen and another door which took you to the walk-in-shower and WC. As I opened the kitchen door, I noticed that someone had helped themselves to food and had used my crockery in the kitchen. I had a new neighbour who recently moved in a few weeks ago and I recall hearing voices and music last night as I drifted off to sleep. It dawned on me that he must have had a party. I went to my bathroom and someone had used my toilet. I felt the anger rise. I allowed the anger to rise and then I suppressed it. I decided to move out of my studio flat. I had been living with inconsiderate people since I moved in and this was the final straw. I did not know where I would live but I just could not stay here any longer. I knew that if I saw my new neighbour, we would have words and I did not trust my mouth as I have had it said to me that I don't have a filter and I know my tongue could be sharp. I called the landlord and I told him what had happened. The landlord said that I do not need to move out and that he would have a talk with the new tenant. Although Mo was lovely and was a good landlord, I had also had enough of the man who lived downstairs with his loud music, parties and drug taking. I had made up my mind to leave. I contacted Pauline and I told her what I had decided to do and why I had made the decision to leave. Pauline said that I could move back into the supported accommodation but she said she was not happy as it seemed like I was going backwards with my progress. I reassured Pauline that this is a temporary set back and that I will soon find alternative accommodation. I knew that this was temporary and I knew that I had to move out. This did not stop me from visualising my dream 3 bedroom house but I was so unsettled. I thanked Pauline for allowing me to reside at the supported accommodation. The only problem I had to overcome now was living and working in the supported accommodation. I moved back into the supported accommodation and I embraced this next chapter of my life. I knew it was not going to be easy as living and working in the same building can be exhausting and can make it hard for one to switch off and focus on my life goals. I used my spare time to visualise my new home. I did not get specific with where I desired to live but all I wanted was to be living in a nice 3 bedroom property with my own garden. I began visualising how I wanted my home to look and I also imagined the feeling of accomplishing it too.

I was working and living at the supported accommodation when one day in August 2015, I received a call from my mum. She told me that Jerry had collapsed whilst he was in his home. Mum said that his partner had called an ambulance and he was taken to hospital. My brother was told that he had a shadow on his lungs and that the doctors had said that it could be one of 3 things; pneumonia, cancer or tuberculosis. My mum was beside herself with worry for my brothers health. My mum said that my brother said he believed that he had cancer. I contacted my brother and spoke with him. He sounded like a man defeated. I encouraged him to be strong and wait until he had a diagnosis but he was focused on the worst outcome. I threw myself in prayer for my brother. I was not worried as my faith in God was strong and I knew God was a good God.

As time went by, my brother became the focus of the family. Some of us rallied around to encourage him to think positive and we showed him love more than ever in his time of need.

I continued to pray for Jerry and I also continued to teach Zumba Fitness and every day, I would actively look for a new home. I would hold my vision of a 3 bedroom house in my imagination and I did not know HOW I would obtain my desired home but I knew it would happen as I obeyed the creative law of our imagination. I kept visualising a 3 bedroom house but as I did not have the finances for such a house, I would go and view 1 bedroom properties and I was always met with resistance. After a lot of frustration, I decided to continue to visualise and I decided to surrender my vision to God. Within a few weeks of being consistent with surrendering my vision to God, there was a huge incident at the supported accommodation. One of the service user's choked on some food as he was intoxicated with drugs and alcohol when he was eating a takeaway meal. Another service user alerted Pauline who ran to help and save the service users life. When the paramedics arrived, the service user was unconscious and was not breathing. Pauline told me to join her in prayer. We both prayed in tongues like our life depended on it. The Paramedics worked on the service user for 35 minutes. At the last minute, they had resuscitated him and whipped him off in the ambulance. The service user was placed on a life support machine and remained in a coma for roughly 4 weeks. We all visited him weekly and spoke to him as if he could hear us. After 4 weeks, the doctors spoke to the service users next of kin about switching the life support machine off as they said he may never recover and if he did then his brain would be severely damaged due to it being starved of oxygen. Pauline pleaded with the service users family to please do not give up. Thankfully, the family member did not give up and within a few days, the service user regained consciousness. He remained in hospital for another few weeks before he was sent home. The service users speech was affected but he was recovering at a miraculous speed. My gratitude was stronger than ever after seeing the power of prayer.

Not too long after the service user incident, I contacted Mo to ask him if he had any vacancies. Mo said that he did have a room in a shared house which was just down the road from the supported accommodation. Mo warned me that I would have to share the communal bathrooms and kitchen with 5 other male tenants. Mo also made me aware that it was not as nice as my previous accommodation that I had left. I decided to take the room as working and living in the same building was not ideal for me. The building of the shared accommodation was old and the rooms were dull and dingy but I had made a choice to move out of the studio flat without planning my next move so I did not complain, instead I held my vision.

I moved in to my new home and whilst it was not my dream home, I was grateful and I counted my blessings one by one. I saw Mo one day as he popped into the shared house to carry out some maintenance jobs. Mo told me that he has a 3 bedroom house but he cannot give me a date as to when it will be available as a lady and her 2 children are living in the house but as the ladies ex-husband sold the house to Mo without letting his ex-wife know, the ex-wife was protesting and refusing to leave her home and so Mo was expecting this to be a long and drawn out court case. Mo also said that I should not hold my breath as he feels it would be easier to offer the lady a tenancy as she had lived in the house for a number of years. I thanked Mo for letting me know. I did not give up on my vision nor did I lust after this house as I understood that to covet another person's belongings is not necessary as what God has planned for me will appear at the appointed time. This did not mean that I must now become complacent, quite the opposite, I visualised consistently every morning and night daily.

One morning I woke up at 5.30am. As I opened my eyes I had received a text message from my brother Jerry. I read the message which read; "Hi Sis, sorry to bother you so early in the morning, but could you please call me when you get this message". I called my brother straight away. Jerry answered the phone. He was shocked that I was awake and was also shocked at how quickly I responded to his text.. My brother called to say that he could not find his TV remote and he was getting upset as he wanted to switch the TV channel over. He began to cry with frustration. I intuitively knew that my brother was scared and this was how he was dealing with it. I managed to calm him down and I asked him if he wanted me to pop over. My brother accepted my invitation. I asked him if he wanted anything from the shops. He asked for a newspaper, some food and drinks. I got up, and got ready to go and visit Jerry.

When I arrived, my brother was a lot calmer than he was on the phone. We sat and spoke and then he asked me to gently massage his back as he said he was in pain. I stayed with my brother until it was time for me to leave to go and take my Saturday morning Zumba Fitness class at 10.00am. When I finished my class, I went home, had a shower, changed my clothes and went back to visit my brother. When I arrived on the afternoon, my brother's friend was with him, and then my mum arrived and one of my younger brothers. My brother was telling us that he is not scared of dying but he said he is terrified of leaving us all behind. There were tears shed by all of us as my brother spoke. I made us all coffee and as I was in my brothers kitchen, I noticed that he had quite a few fridge magnets and key rings that all had messages on about fighting cancer. Because of my new found knowledge of how the mind works and how subliminal messages get in to our hearts, I asked my brother how long had he had a fear of getting cancer. My brother looked me in the eye and said he had feared cancer for many years although he never voiced his fear out loud. I showed my brother a drawing of the stick person presentation and he instantly understood how the fear of cancer had entered into his heart. My brother also confessed that he knew that there was a God and he felt that he needed to humble himself as he reflected on his life. It was a very emotional visit and one that I will remember all the days of my life.

A few weeks later my brother had to go to have an operation in order for the doctors to diagnose the pain in his back and the shadow on his lung. I assisted my brother with attending the consultation appointment where the operation procedure was to be explained to my brother. The consultant showed my brother the x-ray of his lungs and explained the procedure. At no point did the consultant tell my brother that he had cancer but my brother kept asking him if it was cancer. My brother was determined that he had cancer. Once the consultation was over, my brother said he knew he had cancer as his GP at his local surgery had told him that he had cancer and my brother said that his GP had made a claim for terminal illness benefit from the DWP on my brothers behalf. I told my brother not to believe the doctor who assumed he had cancer without doing any tests but my brother was convinced he had the illness.

My brother had his operation and was told that he needs to return to the hospital on the 15th October to get his test results. My brother moved in with one of my cousins who lived near near to my mum's address. I visited my brother as often as I could as did my mom and one of my aunts. One day when I was volunteering, Pauline approached me and said that a tall black man was following me around. Pauline said that she sensed that it was my late grandad. I wasn't alarmed nor was I frightened but I did wonder why I was being followed by my grandad. Pauline asked about Jerry's well-being. I told her the current situation and she said that she wanted to visit him. We arranged with my cousin to visit Jerry. When Pauline and I arrived at my cousin's home, my brother was relaxing on the sofa. Pauline sat with my brother whilst me, my aunt and her daughter were all in the kitchen. After about 30 minutes, Pauline came in to the kitchen and told us that my brother had just given his life to Jesus. I cried with relief. Pauline said that something was going to shock us all in around one weeks time. None of us knew what she was talking about. My cousin decided to monitor my brother by keeping a diary. I visited my brother a couple of times the following week and he appeared to radiate. My brother was in so much pain when he first arrived at my cousin's home but after Pauline's visit, his need for morphine had reduced and he appeared so very peaceful. My aunt said that one day, my brother kept drifting in and out of consciousness and every time he opened his eyes he would say "wow". My aunt said that when she asked Jerry why he was saying wow, she said he just looked at her peacefully and smiled. My aunt said that my brother also cried whilst he was asleep and he was talking about our late grandmother as he said that Pauline reminded him of her.

On October 14th my aunt and I had agreed to attend the hospital with my brother for when he receives his results of the biopsy. We planned what time we would be leaving my cousin's house in order to get my brother there on time for his appointment. I decided to get an early night so that I could be bright eyed and bushy tailed to support my brother tomorrow, as he would be receiving his test results. As I lay my head on my pillow, my cousin called me. She was concerned about my brothers behaviour. My cousin said that she was not sure if he was going blind as he kept bumping into things around her home. I was concerned and so I decided to call Pauline. Pauline spoke to me and reminded me of how God had supernaturally healed me and I was reminded of my astonishing testimonies. Pauline reminded me to trust in God. After our telephone call, I felt very peaceful and assured. I placed my earplugs in and listened to uplifting gospel music as I drifted off to sleep. At 3am on the 15th October, my phone began to ring. I woke up and I was surprised that although I drifted off to sleep with my eye plugs in my ears, the loud ring tone, did not startle me and I woke up relaxed. It was my aunt calling me. I answered the phone. My aunt said that my brother had collapsed on the floor at my cousin's home and that the paramedics were resuscitating him. I quickly jumped out of my bed, threw a coat on and footwear, jumped in my car and headed over to my cousin's house. When I arrived, I saw my brother on the floor being attended to by 2 paramedics. My aunt and cousin were silent. We were all in shock. My aunt later told me that she was present before the paramedics had arrived. She said that as the paramedics worked on resuscitating my brother, my aunt told them to go easy on his chest as he has poorly lungs. My aunt said that one of the paramedics looked at my aunt and said; "this is not his lungs, this is his heart!"

After what seemed like a lifetime, the paramedics said that they had managed to get my brother breathing again and so they quickly put him in the back of the ambulance on a stretcher. I followed the ambulance as they had the blue lights flashing. I kept thinking about the service user who died for 35 minutes who regained consciousness and was now living back at the supported accommodation. I hoped and prayed all the way to the hospital that my brother would regain consciousness and live. I also recall thinking to myself that all things are possible. When I arrived at the main reception I told the receptionist that my brother had just been brought in a few minutes ago. The receptionist knew who I was referring to and directed me to a private side room where she said a doctor would come and let me know any news of my brother. I sat in the room and I felt so lonely and yet so aware that God was with me. I listened to my breathing and the sound of my heart as I waited in silence. After about 10 minutes, the door opened and in walked a doctor. The doctor looked at me and said "I'm so sorry, your brother did not make it". I looked back at the doctor but my brain had not caught up with what I had just heard. I blinked a few times, all the while the doctor looking at me with a warm empathetic glow in his eyes. When I managed to speak I said "thank you for letting me know". The doctor slowly left the room. I was in shock as I just felt numb. I could not accept what I had just heard. Jerry was due to come to this very same hospital today, but not like this, he should have been walking in to the hospital to get his test results not being escorted in on his death bed. Today was the day for us to make a decision on how to move forward with his life but instead, in the next few days we would be planning his funeral. I pictured my big brother in my mind as I whispered to him "why have you left us Jerry?" I was met with silence and a feeling of peace. I gathered my thoughts and set about calling my mum. My mum answered the phone after a couple of rings. I broke the news to her and she cried out from the core of her being. That was one of the most traumatic cries I have ever heard in my life. My mum screamed from the pit of her soul. It was not a nice sound and to me it is unforgettable. I then called my aunt who was in shock. I remained in the private room until one by one, my family arrived. We were all allowed to see my brothers body for the last time before he was to be taken to the chapel of rest. The pain and devastation was obvious on every face as we all said our goodbyes to Jerry. I did not know this yet but after this day of loosing my older brother, my life was going to change in such a way that I could never have comprehended. The next day, I received a call from one of the nurses who knew my brother from his previous hospital visits. The nurse called me and offered her condolences for the loss of Jerry. The nurse said that she was in total shock and she said she could not understand how my brother died. She also kept saying that she could not believe it that he had gone and how shocked her and the team of doctors were at my brothers death. I was too weak to ask her why she was shocked but I knew in my heart why she was shocked, we were all shocked. A few days later my mum called me and told me of some more bad news. A friend who I have known for some time was on holiday and whilst she was away, her brother also passed away. My friend Hannah was devastated and I could relate and emphasise with her loss. We both spoke a few days later and arranged to go out for a drink as our birthday's were only 3 days apart.

CHAPTER 4

NEW BEGINNINGS

We held Jerry's funeral on November 5th in a church that was less than half a mile away from where I lived. Jerry had a good turn out and I was the one who stood before the congregation to read his eulogy. Before the funeral date, I told the family of his favourite song (A little way different by Errol Dunkley) and we played it as the coffin entered the church. It was as if my brother was giving me guidance the day he danced to this song in my car the day he asked me to please pray for him. as to what song he would like played at his funeral.

After my brother was laid to rest, I met up with Hannah on my birthday and we went out to the city centre. Hannah said that she normally celebrated her birthday with lots of friends and family but tonight it was just the 2 of us and I recall it was a lovely night out. Neither of us mentioned our loss as it was still very raw. We enjoyed our night out. I carried on working as a volunteer at the supported accommodation and I continued to teach the Zumba Fitness classes. I kept myself to myself in the shared accommodation and kept my hello's brief and polite. One morning not long after Jerry's funeral, I went to the bathroom to have a shower and I noticed the bath was not clean, someone had also left the toilet with a large brown faeces floating around in the toilet bowl, there was phlegm and pubic hairs in the wash bowl, and there was never any toilet roll in the bathroom. I had cleaning products in my room which I used to clean the bathroom. As I cleaned the bath, my intuition spoke and told me to buy a pack of 6 toilet rolls, some disposable cleaning cloths and some bleach for the toilet. My intuition was very clear and told me to leave a bottle of bleach and one toilet roll in the bathroom. After arguing with the voice of my intuition when he told me to give my brother £50.00, I realised that our intuition knows all things, He doesn't speak just for the sake of speaking, and only guides us in the paths of righteousness for our good and for the good of everyone and everything. I decided to instantly obey. I went out and brought some more bleach, cloths and a pack of 6 toilet rolls. I put one toilet roll on top of the toilet and I left the bottle of bleach by the side of the toilet. The next day, I visited the bathroom and the wash basin had phlegm, pubic hairs, and grime around the basin The toilet roll had disappeared and there was a large brown faeces floating in the toilet bowl. I sighed inwardly and set about cleaning the toilet, sink and bath before I had a shower. I always clean a bathroom before and after I have used it. After I cleaned the bathroom, I went to my room and got another toilet roll out of the packet and I placed it on the top of the toilet. I saw 2 of the other tenants who passed me in the hallway that morning. I said hello and kept walking as I left for work that day. When I arrived back home, I met a tenant who's room was closest to the bathroom. I said hello and he replied "hello sis". I stopped in my tracks as I remembered that this is how Jerry used to address me. I also have 2 younger brother's but they have never called me sis. I felt a tear roll down my cheek as I remembered my brother. The grief was still very raw but day by day I knew the pain would get lighter as long as I did not resist grief and just allow it to express naturally, mainly by allowing myself to cry. I called Pauline who was a good listener sometimes and she allowed me to cry and talk about Jerry when I felt the need to release the pain of loss.

At the shared accommodation, the toilet roll would go missing every day but I chose to listen to the voice of my intuition rather than my rational thinking mind which would advise me to not bother to leave toilet roll in the bathroom as other tenants were taking it out. Mo visited the accommodation and told me that he was sorry to hear of my loss and offered his condolences. We spoke for a few minutes when he mentioned the 3 bedroom house. Mo looked stressed as he explained the hassle he was getting from the lady who was refusing to vacate his house which he had rightfully purchased off her ex husband. I listened to Mo as he spoke but due to the pain of loosing my brother, my desire to move out of the shared accommodation was not as strong as it had been in the past. Mo said that I mustn't hold my breath of living in the 3 bedroom property as he did not know what was going to happen with the lady who was refusing to give up her home. Mo also said something along the lines of offering the lady a tenancy as she clearly did not want to leave her home where she lived with her 2 children.

The following day I was down to my last toilet roll but I decided to stay strong in my faith and take it to the bathroom. I arrived at the bathroom and stopped dead in my tracks. The sink was spotless and clean, the toilet was cleaned with the bleach and there on the shelf were 3 toilet rolls. As if by magic, the bathroom was left so clean and tidy. My persistence and patience had paid off. I whispered "thank you" to my intuition and I felt a huge wave of love and acceptance. I walked back to my room when I heard the front door open. It was Mo. He was smiling as he said "Kate, I went to the 3 bedroom property to speak with the lady and when I arrived, she had packed all of her things and she has left". Mo said he could not believe it and he has no idea how this could have happened. Mo told me that I could have first offer on the house. He also told me that I would need to pay £1,100.00 which is made up of one months rent upfront and a deposit of £550.00. I agreed to view the property. It was breath taking. The living room was huge as was the 3 bedrooms. The house was spacious with a huge front and back garden. The house was situated quite far back away from the main road. All of the fixtures and fittings were new and modern. The bathroom had a huge P shaped bath and newly fitted sink units. The kitchen had new fitted worktops and cupboards. The front door and windows were about 6 months old and they looked very expensive. Mo had taken great pride in replacing radiators and he also fitted wooden flooring and placed new doors with expensive brass door handles in every room. My intuition told me to make a decision without looking at my present financial state. I felt courageous and so I decided to accept Mo's offer. I went home and prayed about the deposit and the first months rent. My intuition said you will move in on the 30th November 2015. I trusted my intuition more than anyone or any situation. I have unshakable faith as I am aware that our intuition is always 100% right all of the time, after all, our intuition is the voice of God.

On the 30th November 2015, I met Mo at the property. Mo handed me the keys to my dream home. Mo asked for the money, I looked him in the eye and I told him that I do not have the money but I really want to live here. Mo looked at me with compassion in his eyes and he did not argue with me and he said OK, but you have to give me some kind of financial payment.. We both went silent. I felt embarrassment rise as I waited for Mo to speak. Eventually Mo spoke and said, "I can take one weeks rent off you today and we will sort out a payment plan how you can make the payments to catch up with the rent". Mo calculated one weeks rent which came to £126.92. I did not know how much money I had in my purse and when I emptied my purse, I counted £127.02. I thanked Mo for allowing me to live in my dream home and I gave Mo one weeks rent. When he left I walked around my home in awe. Although the house was empty as I had no furniture, I did not let it concern me. I sat down on a bean bag that was left in the house by the previous owner and I spoke to God. I thanked Him for His love and mercy, I thanked Him for Mo. My intuition prompted me to sit down and work out a payment plan to get out of debt. Once I had done this, I contacted Mo to ask him if he was willing to accept my monthly offers. Mo is so lovely and not like other landlords I have heard about. He is very understanding and professional. From this day, Mo and I became friends and we have communicated with each other regularly from this day.

I was so grateful that I was now living in a beautiful home. I met my neighbours briefly and settled in. I kept myself to myself and so did my neighbours. Whenever we saw each other we would politely say hello and keep it moving.

I continued to work at the supported accommodation and I remained under the mentorship of Pauline. We would have 1-2-1 sessions and Pauline would monitor my personal development and if I was going in the wrong direction with my thoughts, she would correct me and put me back on the path of success. Pauline gifted me a single bed, a 20" flat screen TV, a washing machine and a coffee table and took me to a department store where she brought me some beautiful curtains, lampshades and cushions. One of Pauline's daughters had recently brought a house which was partly furnished. Before Pauline's daughter, Sonia had brought her new house, she had brought a beautiful grey corner sofa but when she moved in to her new house, there was a brand new sofa which matched her living room so she decided to gift me the one she had previously brought. I offered her money but she would not accept any money from me and told me it was a gift from her. One of my younger sisters gifted me a black 2 seater leather chair and a vacuum cleaner. I decided to invest in SKY as I needed internet and I enjoyed the extra TV channels. SKY had a black Friday offer where they were giving away 32" TV's for first time subscribers. I called SKY to have broadband, the TV services and a landline and I was given a new 32" TV too. My new home was being furnished by acts of love from other people. It is an amazing feeling to be loved and it is just as amazing to be able to give love towards others without a motive too. I settled in my new home and continued to work at Pauline's supported accommodation and my Zumba Fitness classes started to grow nice and steadily. Within 6-12 months, my home was becoming more cosy and comfortable. I had managed to buy a double bed from a lady who was selling it on a social media platform. The mattress was new and still had the plastic covering and the bed frame was made of solid oak wood. It was a very attractive bed and I got it at a bargain. Pauline also gave me a 2 month old 40" TV and so I donated £250.00 to Pauline's supported accommodation.

CHAPTER 5

THE GENUINE CRY OF A SOUL

As I settled in to my new home, I was at ease with life. I was still coming to terms with the loss of my older brother. Life seemed strange without him. I had good days and not so good days when something would remind me of him. I think the worst time was when I heard something from reading a news article online. I recall thinking "I must call Jerry and tell him about this". I picked up my phone and as I unlocked it and went to call my brother, the realisation of my brother no longer here, hit me like a ton of bricks. I kept repeating to myself that Jerry has gone, I cannot believe that I will never see my brother again".

As time went by, I improved my home with some new furniture and I enjoyed going to work and returning to a quiet home. I also made some lovely friends with some of the ladies from my Zumba Fitness classes. We met up at Christmas and also had nights in at my home where the laughter could be heard throughout my home. I had dated 2 men but I never dated them for longer than a few weeks. I was deeply missing Mike and I decided to pray to God. I mentioned my relationship to one of my Zumba ladies whom I had become really good friends with. Her name was Shelly and she told me that it sounds like Mike was my soulmate and that she believed that we will meet up again one day. I really wanted to believe her but I had no way of contacting him and I would not know where to start looking for him. The pain of loosing my brother and missing Mike would overwhelm me some days but I never stayed down for long, as I would brush myself down and get on with living life.

I went through 2016 missing my brother and I took each day as it came. I laughed some days and I also cried some days. I found it difficult coming to terms of loosing Jerry. I continued to work at the supported accommodation and I continued being mentored by Pauline. I also spent most nights wondering how Mike was fairing in life. I was sure that he would have moved on and I told myself that he is probably happy and settled with a new partner. I found myself wondering what my life would be like if we were still together. Most days I would find myself visualising that I was happy in love with the perfect man of my dreams. I did not picture Mike, but I sensed his warm loving presence and I embraced the feeling of being loved.

I spent a lot of time with Hannah as she did not live too far from me. We went out some weekends and the laughs we had are remembered to this day. Hannah has lots of stories to tell about my driving skills and my fear of crawling insects and flying ones too.

I also spend time with some of the ladies that attended my Zumba Fitness sessions. The laughs we had were really good for the soul. I was surrounded by great women and this helped me a lot as I truly believe that your environment is the key foundation of how we experience life.

It was January 2017 and one day I was sat eating my evening meal. After my meal, I contemplated my testimonies and I dwelt on how my life was miraculous. I thought about the love of God towards me and how I could not comprehend God's mercy. I got up from my seat and walked to the kitchen with my dinner plate. I spontaneously began to scream at God. The cry came from the core of my soul. I shouted by saying; "Who are you that keeps on blessing me and blessing me and blessing me? And who am I? If you don't tell me who I am and who YOU are, then you had better take me off this earth as I cannot live another day with this huge empty void inside of my soul!" I went silent and then I cried. I had been praising God and seeing the hand of God in my life but I could not live another day not truly knowing who He was and who I was. I knew God spoke to me through my intuition but there was much more to God than this. I just knew that there was a depth that was deep and I knew that God was almighty. I knew I was not just a mortal body, but I could not comprehend who I was as I would see different facets to my personality and this threw me and made me feel vulnerable. I sometimes felt trapped and confused about life. I read the Bible, went to church, had fellowship with other believer's, I understood deep truths in the Bible but yet, I knew something was missing and all I wanted was the absolute truth. About 2 minutes after my outburst, my mentor randomly sent me a video via a social media platform. I clicked on the link and watched a video of a man named Mooji. As I listened to him, I realised that he knew the absolute truth about life. This man was deep and this new information I was hearing is not for the mind, it was for the human spirit, the spirit that knows it is not immortal and who knows and who is one with the deep truth on life.

Every day as I watched and listened to Mooji, I knew that I had stumbled on a greater truth and it also dawned on me that I may have opened up a can of worms as my life was to fall apart before it would be put back together again. I spent day and night listening to and watching Mooji on YouTube. The more I listened the more confused my psychological mind became but at the same time, the more stable and peaceful I felt inside at a deeper level. This continued and as if by magic, I began to get clarity on the truth of life. I had stumbled on teachings that could only be experienced as words did not really do it much justice. I continued to listen to Mooji and I felt that I had to allow Mooji's words to penetrate my soul and I started to experience that all of my deep seated beliefs were melting away as I was left with clarity and great peace. I began to notice how peaceful, harmonious and meaningful my relationships were becoming, and I felt waves of love when I interacted with people. Life was dancing and I was realising that I am the dancer. Some days my mind would get noisy and some days I would experience great peace. It would seem that I was slowly waking up to my true nature and I recognised that it was a process and I also recognised that I felt lighter and happier.

I recall one day at the beginning of August 2017, I felt a strong urge to be with Mike. Over the years I had suppressed my pain of splitting up with him but as I did this deeper work, the pain became more frequent and stronger. I was now on a new journey of self discovery and enlightenment and I felt my intuition prompt me to pray about Mike. I wrote down all the things I loved about him and I asked my intuition to please bring us back together if we were meant to be. The pain and frustration was so unbearable, and I spoke to one of the ladies from the Zumba Fitness class called Nancy who I became very close to. Nancy would listen to me as I spoke fondly of Mike and she said that if it is meant to be, then we would be back together. Nancy said that she had a good feeling about Mike and I and she urged me to keep my faith and not to give up.

On 30th August 2017, I received a prayer via social media and I decided to pray this prayer and pass it on as suggested by the sender. I prayed the prayer earnestly and sent it to one of my younger sister's. The prayer was a one minute prayer and was very powerful. I felt a shift of positive energy in my core after I prayed. Later that day, I received a text message from a service user. When I got the notification, I remembered the text messages that Mike always sent me daily. I responded to the service user who had sent me a text message and then I had an intuitive thought. I typed Mike's name in my search bar on my messages and all of a sudden, my phone had a 3 year memory of all the messages that Mike had sent me. I screamed and dropped my phone! I had completely forgotten that Mike had another mobile number that he use to contact me on back in 2012 when we first met. I picked up my phone and I went into the messages. They were from 2013!! I began to read the messages and I realised that this was not the phone number that I had blocked and deleted back in 2014. I was shaking and trembling with excitement and fear. I decided to send a message to this number. I wrote something along the lines of "Hello Mike, it's Kate. I hope you are OK? and I just wanted to let you know that I have missed you xxx". I then called my friend Nancy to tell her the news. Nancy said that I should call him but I told her no as he could be busy working. Later that day, I had a Zumba Fitness session at 7.30 pm. Nancy attended the class and at the end of the class she asked me if I had received a reply off Mike. I told her that I had not but I had a certainty in my soul that we would be re-connected and I decided to patiently wait for him to reply as I just knew that he would. Nancy smiled and said to me that she knew we would be re-united and she offered to call his number. Nancy asked for Mike's number and I gave it to her. Nancy called Mike's phone and it began to ring! Nancy quickly disconnected the call and smiled at me saying "Well, at least we know the number is active my lovely". Nancy and I stood in a car park near the gym and spoke for roughly 15 minutes before we said our goodbye's. As I drove home, I was so excited and I had

133

a warm fuzzy feeling in my heart. I just knew that Mike and I would get back together. Later on that evening, I was sat eating my meal and Nancy called me. She was screaming with excitement down the phone as she said a man had just called her asking who she was as he had a missed call from her mobile number. As I was on the phone to Nancy, I received a text message, it was from Mike.

My hands shook as I read the text message. Mike had replied to my message saying; "Hello lovely Kate, I remember you well, it's nice to hear from you xx". I quickly sent another message and before I knew it, we were texting each other for around 2 hours and we arranged to meet up on Saturday night. That night as I lay in my bed, I had lots of thoughts in my mind and I could not believe that after 3 years, I had finally been reconnected with the love of my life, my soulmate, Mike.

The rest of the week passed and then finally Saturday had arrived. I met Mike near his parents house and as soon as our eyes met, I knew this was fate. I drove us to my home, as I drove, we talked as if we had never been apart. The chemistry was there and the conversation was flowing with ease. Mike and I spent the evening together and the love between us was evident. Mike was working in another city down South but said that he would be visiting every Friday. We picked up our relationship, where we had left off. Mike told me that he also knew that we would be together again and said that he could not date another woman since we split in 2014 as he said that he had fallen deeply in love with me. I felt the same. I explained to Mike that I was upset as I thought he did not feel affection towards me. I also told him that I was sorry for ending our relationship back in 2014. Mike was a little upset as he said that we have lost 3 years and that he knew that I was the one for him when we met back in 2012. We made up and we both knew that we would be together forever as we both loved each other and our relationship was pure. I had no trust issues with Mike and he said the same to me. Mike and I got on really well, we had a strong bond, we respected each other, there was no control and we gave each other space to breathe.

I continued to work at the supported accommodation and do the Zumba Fitness sessions and Mike and I grew closer and closer day by day. I also continued on the path of enlightenment and I found myself understanding Mooji's words a lot easier as I listened to his pointing's day after day and night. I also found another spiritual leader called Eckhart Tolle. Both Eckhart and Mooji were saying the same thing and it was just a matter of translation but they were both profound master's of life. I did meditation practices and self-enquiry 2-3 times a day as I went deeper I found that my old belief system was completely falling apart as I self realised the truth of life. All that I had learned over the past few years of delving into personal development, and Christianity had crumbled and I found reading the Bible with so much understanding and enlightenment. This is where the Bible really became alive and I could fully comprehend Jesus' words and teachings. I also had the realisation of all religions and I could clearly see that we are all of one race, the human race.

As I continued to work at Pauline's supported accommodation, I found that there had been a relationship breakdown between Pauline and I. I found her quite difficult to work with and I found that she believed that she was always in the right. I respected her as a mentor but she was presenting as arrogant and I was finding it impossible to be around her. The way she spoke to me and others was not acceptable and I often felt undermined and belittled. I continued to listen to Mooji and Eckhart and the more I comprehended there teachings, the more I found it very difficult to be around Pauline's behaviour. One day in November 2017, I decided that this lady was stuck in her ways and was not willing to budge so I made a decision to walk away from the supported accommodation. I walked out of my day job and I went into solace at home where I spent the next 2 weeks listening to Mooji, studying Mooji and falling in love with his teachings. I would wake up at 7am and spend the whole day listening to and comprehending his powerful words. I felt that I needed to do this and I was not overly concerned about having a monthly salary. I decided to put all my trust in to God. My monthly bills were due to be paid in a few days and I recall my thoughts around this. I was calm and assured that all is well and it turned out to be so. My bills were paid and the bills where the funds were not available I contacted the debtors who all seemed to be OK with the fact that they may not be paid this month and some companies said that they would waver my bill. I experienced life flowing and it was unexplainable and I realised how fragile my old beliefs were.

After spending 2 weeks at home and in solace, my landlord Mo contacted me asking if I would work for him as he also had properties that were used to house vulnerable adults who had identified support needs and he said he needed a support worker who could start ASAP. After 2 weeks of being at home alone, I was thankful for the opportunity and I felt I was ready to test what I had learned from listening to Mooji whilst in solace.

CHAPTER 6

DEVASTATION

It was mid November and I got ready to start my new job working as a full-time support worker. In my previous job, I was stationed at one supported accommodation and so I was able to meet the support needs of the service user's all under one roof. Mo had 2 properties in the same area and he was in the process of opening a 3rd supported accommodation in another area which was roughly 3 miles away. I found that the service user's needs were not as complex as the ones I had previously worked with but I found my role equally as challenging as most of the time, some service users did not want to engage with the offered support. Mo was brilliant and supported me as I learned the ropes. Mo sent me on training and I began to realise how important it was to understand how to support the service users. As time went by, I began to form a system where I was able to manage the support plans and make time for the service users. As the weeks passed, the role got easier and I was making progress with encouraging the service users to engage with the offered support. In one property, there were 2 room vacancies and I was required to fill both rooms. I did this by contacting agencies and sending out referral forms. Within a few days, both of the properties were full. I continued to teach Zumba Fitness classes some evenings at a local gym and this helped me immensely as I would dance away any stress I felt in my body due to my day job.

Before I knew it, it was fast approaching Christmas. Most of the service users told me that they would spend Christmas with their family and friends but there were 3 service users that said they would be spending Christmas alone. Due to Mike working away and working throughout Christmas, he came home on Christmas Eve where we celebrated our Christmas together as he had to return to work the next day. I was able to pop in to see the 3 service users on Christmas Day before I made my way to my parents house to spend Christmas with my family. It was pretty much the same scenario on New Years Eve where the service users' were concerned.

2018 had arrived and I reflected on life. I knew I had a purpose but my vision was not yet clear. I remained under the teachings of Mooji and listened attentively to his pointing's and his great wisdom. I am not going to say that it was easy to digest some of Mooji's wisdom but it was causing my conscious mind to align with a greater truth. I felt peaceful most of the time but my phycological mind would appear to be really noisy some days but Mooji pointed out that this is a natural process in his Satsang meditation groups. I found that by doing the self enquiry practices, my life became peaceful and I was able to take on more work without being overwhelmed.

In March, the new supported accommodation had passed its inspection and so now, I am working in two area's and I embraced this change. As soon as we opened the new property, we had it filled with 5 service users in 24 hours. I was very busy supporting the service users' with settling them in and I really enjoyed my role as a support worker.

By May, I had taken on 2 new service users' who had complex mental health illness and high support needs. One was a male and the other was a female. Both service users engaged well with me and I found this easier as I worked in partnership with NHS and Adult Social Services. The only challenge I found was that the 2 service users' were in 2 different properties and so for this reason I made a decision to start my job 1 hour earlier so that I could offer them both support in the morning before 10am. It dawned on me how vulnerable some of the service users were. As time went by, some of the service users who were at the properties when I first started my role, had moved out and the service users' that replaced them were all suffering with a mental health condition. I decided to take online courses so that I could understand the needs of the service users that I supported. As I studied each evening, I felt a huge desire to do more for vulnerable service users. Was this my purpose? It most certainly kept me wondering as I lay in bed some nights.

Working as a support worker is a very rewarding role in today's society but I witnessed devastation too. Whilst I worked in an are where there were over 300 properties that offered supported accommodation, I saw vulnerable adults taking drugs and being placed in the back of ambulances. I watched predator's target the most vulnerable, I watched and learned how some landlords treated their service users', I witnessed exploitation and brutality. I found myself safeguarding the service users by working in partnership with social services, probation officers, the police and the NHS. I did safeguarding workshops and goal setting workshops with some of the service users and they proved to be successful with a handful of service users, but the problem in supported accommodation on a whole remained. This was too much pain for my soul, I cried out to God in prayer to please help the vulnerable and to please give me a solution. Not long after my prayer, I saw a huge house one day and an idea sprung to my mind. I thought that if I could have a huge house to provide robust support packages then maybe I could be the solution but I knew that it was going to be a long and rocky road but it was a road I had to endure not only for the vulnerable but also to find peace in my soul.

I continued working for Mo as a support worker and my personal life was becoming balanced as was my relationship with Mike which blossomed daily. The more I sat under the teachings of Mooji and Eckhart Tolle, the more I was becoming enlightened on life and my purpose was becoming clearer. All of my relationships became harmonious and life seemed peaceful. Mike and I grew closer daily and we spoke of getting married but we had not set a definite date as it was just something we spoke about.

In July of 2018, I received a referral from a psychiatric ward where the staff were looking for suitable accommodation for one of the female patients who was ready to be discharged from hospital. I attended the ward to do a risk assessment on the patient. The patient was named Lucy and she said that she would like to take on a tenancy with the landlord for the supported accommodation. I was happy to support Lucy and so she became one of our female service users. Lucy was a heroin addict and presented as vulnerable. Lucy was a lovely lady but I could see that her soul was lost as she had endured trauma and was taking each day as it came. Lucy settled in well and had a very gentle soul which was hidden behind the power of addiction. Lucy was a resident for just over 2 weeks when I received a phone call one evening from one of the male service users who shared the house where Lucy also lived. I can recall that evening as if it was yesterday. I was sat watching TV eating my meal when my mobile phone rang. When I saw who was calling me, I immediately answered the call as this service user never complained or bothered anyone and he was not the type of person to call me out of work hours unless it was an emergency. I listened as the service user shouted down the phone. He was telling me that he was not happy as someone had stolen his food from the fridge which was in the communal kitchen. I listened as he was clearly upset and although this was not classed as an emergency, I knew that the service user needed to vent his frustration. The service user said that he had a gut feeling that Lucy had stolen his food and that he was going to confront her when she returned as she was not currently indoors. The service user said that he had no money to buy a meal and so I told him that I would gather some tins from my cupboard and bring him some food this evening. The service user calmed down and hung up. I continued to eat my meal. Two minutes later, the service user called me again. I answered my phone. This time he spoke with fear in his voice as he told me that Lucy's siblings had arrived at the supported accommodation as they had received news that Lucy was dead and so they arrived at her accommodation to see if she was there as they did not want to believe the news they had received early that day. I told the service user that I am on my way and I began to grab my handbag and keys to go to the supported accommodation which was a 10 minute drive from my home. I called Mo and told him about the phone call and he also made his way to the property. When I arrived, Mo was standing outside of the property speaking with 2 of the service users but there was no sign of Lucy's siblings. Mo asked me if I would please check Lucy's room. I hesitated but then I recall feeling courageous and so I knocked on Lucy's door and there was no answer. I looked through the bunch of keys that I had and when I found the key for Lucy's room, I slowly turned the key in the lock. I looked at Mo who was looking back at me with fear on his face. I entered the room and it was neat and tidy but no sign of Lucy. The service user who had called me earlier to complain about having his food stolen handed me a piece of paper which Lucy's siblings had given him with a mobile phone number written on it and a few words which read "Please call me if my sister comes home". I stared at the paper and decided to call the number to speak with Lucy's sibling. As the phone rang, I recall my heart beating loud in my chest. Lucy's sister answered the phone. I told her who I was and I asked her what was going on. Lucy's sister explained to me that earlier that day, she was told by a local shop keeper that a rumour was going around that Lucy had died in another drug users flat. Lucy's sister said that as she had not seen her sister that day, she became worried and decided to go to the supported accommodation hoping to find her sister at home. Lucy's sister told me that she was at the local police station making a missing person's report. I instinctively knew that something was not quite right with this story and so I decided to call the police as I would also need to file a missing persons report. The police took information from me regarding Lucy's personal details and gave me a log number. Some of the service users that were at the property were disturbed, frightened and concerned for Lucy's safety so Mo and I decided to stay with them for 2 hours to assure them that the police are doing all they can do to find Lucy but I knew deep down that Lucy was never going to come back home.

It was 10.30pm when I arrived back home and I could not settle. I called Pauline as I needed to speak with someone about anything to distract my mind. Pauline was very supportive and encouraged me to pop in and visit her at her office which was in the supported accommodation that she ran. After I spoke with Pauline, I decided to call Lucy's sister to ask if she had any news. Lucy's sister spoke to me and confirmed my fears... Lucy was found dead in another drug users flat earlier this morning. After I had spoken with Lucy's sister, I called Mo to let him know.

A note from the Author

As soon as I had heard that Lucy may have passed away and that the circumstances were drug related, it reminded me of the devastation I had escaped from substance misuse. Lucy was someone's daughter, mother, sibling and friend. Lucy never had much in terms of material items but what she had was a heart of gold. I knew her soul was troubled and I knew she attempted to hide behind the mask of addiction and a smile that didn't quite reach her eyes. I later found out that

Lucy had died of heroin overdose and someone had helped Lucy inject heroin into her veins as I learned that Lucy could not inject heroin and needed someone to help her do it. The pain and anguish her family endured was unspeakable. I visited Lucy's family with Lucy's belongings and a bunch of flowers. I comforted Lucy's grieving mother as I understood the devastation of drug addiction. I genuinely hope that people who may have an addiction, find the hope, courage and determination to reach out to others who can help and support them in their hour of need.

As time went by, I continued to work as a support worker. In October 2018, Mo opened another supported accommodation and I helped him to make the property homely for the new service users. I was visualising running one property to support service users who needed extra support due to their complex support needs. This vision was getting clearer each time I spent time visualising but I just could not see how it would be possible. I had no savings and I had no idea how to do this. Mike was very supportive and encouraged me to keep going in the direction I was going in as he said I have a gift to help vulnerable people become empowered with hope of a better future. The nights I cried to Mike about the pain I felt as I watched vulnerable adults suffer due to the lack of care and support in supported accommodation. I often spoke with Pauline and I visited her from time to time.

One night I was visualising about running a house for the extremely vulnerable. After I finished visualising I decided to call Pauline. We spoke and I told her about my vision. When Pauline heard what I said, she said to me "Your vision sounds like what I offer at the supported accommodation so why don't you come back?". Before I left working for Pauline in 2017, we both vowed that we would not work with each other again due to conflict. Pauline remained as my mentor and we got on much better, we kept our relationship as mentor and student. Pauline had taught me so much over the years and I always had a warm heart towards her. I even called her Mum when I addressed her, but we just could not work together as we frustrated each other, our personalities clashed far too much.

Later that evening, I sat and I kept seeing a vision of running Pauline's supported accommodation and my heart felt content. I visualised the service users' being happy to receive the right care and support and I also thought of Mo and how I would tell him that I am leaving my position as support worker to be a contractor and I will be returning to Pauline's supported accommodation. I thought of how much easier it would be for the service users' to all be under the same roof so that I could be there for them all without having to visit multiple properties. I know this may sound like I abandon people and positions, but I follow my heart and this was not a selfish desire, it was a calling on my soul.

Pauline and I spoke over the phone about me returning as a contractor. I made it clear to her that I must do this on my own as we cannot work together. Pauline said that she was retiring and had no desire to interfere with my position as a contractor. I thought it would be in a few months but Pauline said that she was stepping away from the supported accommodation on 1st February 2019 which was only weeks away. Pauline contacted me to discuss the way forward and for me to read and sign the contract. I told Mo about my plans. Mo said he was happy for me as he knew this was what I had always wanted but he was a little upset that I was leaving and at such short notice. Mo and I worked well together, we never had any conflict and he always supported me with my role bur he also knew that I had always desired to have a huge house to offer support to the vulnerable.

February 1st 2019 arrived. Before I left for my first day as a contractor, I looked at myself in the mirror on my bedroom wall, and I said out loud, "Girl, you can do this!" I arrived at Pauline's supported accommodation and got settled in. I was a little overwhelmed as the work ahead looked daunting but I had learned over the years that all things are possible and I knew this decision I had made was a step in the right direction. I kept my focus on the bigger picture and I never allowed doubt to slip in and destroy my vision.

As the weeks passed, I got into the swing of things. There were a few teething problems to begin with but I soon found my feet. I was on the path to fulfilling my hearts desire. I managed to get new service users' from psychiatric wards, social services referrals and from the probation services. Since leaving Pauline in 2017 and working for Mo, I had partnered with the community mental health team (CMHT), the police, social services, the homeless services, and other service providers. Most of the service users' had complex support needs and I loved the challenges. I loved helping the service users overcome their challenges. My main area of expertise was safeguarding and preventing incidents. I made some fantastic connections with other professionals as we joined in partnership to work together to support the service users to achieve their best possible outcome. I worked hard, I dotted all I's and crossed all the T's. My only real challenge was Pauline. She did not stick to her side of the contract and would interfere with the work I was doing. I understood that she was the licence holder and that she was the overall decision maker but she did not make my role easy as she would call me some days and ask me to attend to her personal affairs. I politely told her that I am not her personal assistant and that she is distracting me from running the supported accommodation. Everything was running smooth, the service users were engaging with the support and they always paid their service charges on time. I made sure that all of the service users' were safeguarded and all of their support needs were met. I had to make decisions based on my experience and the current legislation but because Pauline was use to making her decisions on a whim, we began to clash again. Pauline was not co-operating and I recall one incident that made me see the woman who I called my mentor in a different light.

I had managed to fill the house with service users and everyone of them happily paid their service charges. Pauline decided that they should be paying more money and she instructed me to speak with some of the service users about the huge increase. I did not feel comfortable with this and I reminded Pauline about our conversation we had in January when I told her how much I will be collecting off the service users, but because she could see how well they paid and the fact they paid on time without any problems, Pauline was going to ask for an extra £200.00. Now, I just want to make something clear. If Pauline could justify the extra money by providing a service that is worthy of the extra £200.00 then I would have agreed but she spoke about how much she was paying me and said that the service users should contribute more of their money. The frustrating thing was that as Pauline was making demands that I carry out duties that had nothing to do with running the supported accommodation, she was sapping my time and energy which was hindering the quality and level of support that I could offer the service users. I was not happy about this decision and I told her that if she was going to request more money from the service users without adding any value to their current support needs then she would need to come in and personally request this money from them herself. She kept telling me about her eligible and ineligible service charges and to be quite honest, most of it was going over my head. I sat down and worked out how much income was coming in and then I looked at how much the company was paying out each month. The company was making a profit and I often helped with tithing in to the company but Pauline was still determined to request more money from the service users. Pauline arranged to come in to see the service users and asked me to please be present. I agreed but it was only so that I could support the service user. Pauline arranged to come in at 12 noon one day and she asked me to please have some of the service users relevant documents ready for when she saw them. She also asked me to let the service users know that she was visiting them and she made appointments with each one. I was ready and waiting for Pauline to arrive and so were the service users. I patiently waited and I apologised to the 3 service users who were becoming increasingly anxious as they waited to have their meeting with Pauline. I felt frustration rise as the clock ticked. It was almost 1pm and I was getting ready to go and have my lunch as I had been in work since 8.30am and I had not eaten since having my breakfast at 6.30am. Pauline arrived at 12.55pm and she demanded that I join her in the meetings. There was no appology, no regard for me or the service users and it was obvious that she was in a bad mood. I felt the anger rise and I told her that she is rude! Pauline began to raise her voice and she kept on calling me illiterate over and over and over. Pauline's time keeping was really bad, and I am not always the best time keeper but I always contact people and make them aware that I am going to be late, but Pauline was so arrogant as she just waltzed in and made demands on everyone to fall into line with her. After she insulted me, I picked up my coat and belongings and I left. I was so angry I had tears in my eyes. I called Joanne who was know for being diplomatic and she was the daughter who I went with to take the Zumba Fitness course back in 2012. Joanne listened as I told her about the issue. Joanne was lovely and she understood that her mum could be difficult and she even said so herself. I told her that I am ending my contract as I cannot work with her mum. Joanne calmed me down and spoke to me about the benefits of working with the service users and how I was doing a great job. She also said that she would be speaking with her mum too. After speaking with Joanne, I calmed down and I returned to Pauline's supported accommodation. When I returned, Pauline was speaking with Joanne on the phone. I went into the office and I carried on with my work. Pauline did not manage to have her meetings with the service users as I did not want to be in the same room as her and it is not professional to attend meetings with hostility. Pauline left after an hour or so and I continued to support the service users and when it was 5pm, I left to go home. I spoke with Mike and I told him about my day. He listened and comforted me but I knew he was annoyed as he did not like Pauline and all he kept saying was that he wanted me to be happy in my role. Later that evening, Pauline contacted me to apologise for her behaviour and she said that she was uneasy with the fact that I could not approach her with my issues. I was dumbfounded by this statement. I really do not think that Pauline was aware of her attitude and the way she chose to speak to others. She did not acknowledge that she caused the whole disagreement with her attitude.

A few days later, Pauline came in to meet with the service users to make them aware that she wanted more money off them as they were receiving the correct benefits. One of the service users did not understand why they were being asked to pay more but due to their vulnerability, they agreed. One service user who was recently discharged from a psychiatric ward in February, protested and turned to me in anger. He had just began to gain trust in me and this meeting had shattered that trust. This service user was placed in hospital as he had attempted suicide and since being discharged and in to my care, he was making progress as he utilised emotional and practical support. On the evening I received a call from one of the service users telling me that he had attempted suicide and that the paramedics were on their way. I drove to the supported accommodation and when I arrived, the service user looked distressed. I spoke with him and he said that something in him still trusts me but he did not like Pauline as he felt that she was talking down at him and that he did not want to stay at the accommodation any longer. I listened and I told him that I do not want him to leave and that we could work something out to help him on the road to recovery. He looked me in the eye and said that he is really willing to engage but he never wants to see Pauline again. The paramedics took the service user to hospital and I left to go back home. Over the next few weeks, this service user became non verbal and would only speak to me. He was so sweet and misunderstood. He protested about the extra charges but said because he loved me, he would pay. I knew that this was not right so I made an application to Adult Social Services to speak with them about funding his care and support needs and his identified vulnerabilities. I worked in partnership with the service users CPN, psychiatrist and his social worker. My goal was to make sure that everyone benefited. I was diligent at providing support to the service users, I always ensured that they paid their service charges and I ran a tight ship but it seemed that Pauline was never satisfied and would throw spanners in the works just as I got everything back in order. Another service user decided to leave as he was settled and was doing really well until Pauline hit him with a service charge increase. Pauline was having a negative impact on all of our lives but she seemed to be totally oblivious.

Mike was very supportive and he often comforted me when I had a hard day due to clashing with Pauline. Mo was also very supportive too. Mo and I had grown closer as friends and often spoke over the phone several times a day. Mo had become my support network alongside CPN's and some social workers. Everyone was supporting me to carry on as they said that they could see huge improvements in the service users well-being. Mike met Mo one day as Mo needed to attend my home to do a repair and Mike said that he seemed like a nice person. Due to Mike being a specialist in his field, one of his abilities was that he could read people and situations very quickly. Mike was non judgemental and had a way of sensing and feeling peoples motives. He said he trusted Mo around me and that was mainly because he knew I was faithful and trustworthy. Mike said he had no issues with Mo but he often said that he felt men would not resist me given half the chance. I had the Zumba ladies too, they were very supportive. Everyone was cheering me on except Pauline. My heart felt heavy as I really loved this lady. She had been so kind to me when I first arrived at her supported accommodation back in 2011. Mike said that he felt that I had outgrown Pauline and he often said that he felt that I had a false sense of loyalty towards her. Mike often said that I owed her nothing as I also made huge contributions to her project. I knew Mike did not like Pauline after the incident back in 2012 but I always ask him to attempt to forgive and forget. Mike always encouraged me to go after my goal, keep my focus and keep on being me. I really had an amazing partner and close friends.

My birthday was fast approaching and Mike asked me what I wanted for a birthday present I had everything I needed and so I could not think of anything specific. Mike looked at my hands and said that he would like to buy me a ring. I gave him my ring size as I thought he would buy me a nice dress ring. Mike brought me a beautiful engagement ring! We did not set a date for our wedding as Mike said that he intends to spend the rest of his life with me and said he is not in a rush to get married but he often called me his wife. Mike and I grew closer and closer. Our love was pure. We spent most weekends together snuggled up on the sofa with a takeaway, a good movie and beverages. When Mike left on Sunday afternoon to return to London, I missed him but I was never lonely. I continued to listen to Mooji on YouTube and my conscious awareness was growing more and more. I was still faced with challenges but I was learning not to identify with them. I spent a lot of time turning my attention inwards as I focused on the stillness within. I noticed that as I practiced what I had learned from Mooji, my relationships, finances, career, environment and emotions were becoming balanced and a sense of well-being was very evident from within. I became more intuitive and responsive to the voice of my intuition. I recall going grocery shopping one day in May and having a strong urge to spend over £150.00 on cleaning products, toilet rolls, hand sanitizer and latex gloves. I had no idea why I went on such a spending spree. Mike said that I may have an obsessive compulsory disorder (OCD) but I dismissed this as I knew my intuition moves me to do unusual things and I had learned to go with the flow of life.

CHAPTER 7

LOCK DOWN

Christmas 2019 was over before I knew it and I invited my immediate family over to my home for a Boxing Day meal. Mike was away working but I still managed to enjoy the Christmas season with my loved ones. My family also commented on the amount of cleaning products and toilet roll that they saw in my outhouse and cupboards. I think they also thought that I had OCD. One day in January, I was stood in my kitchen preparing a meal when I heard my intuition speak; "There will be famine but do not fear". I had to ask myself if what I just heard was true. Famine, in 2020? I continued to prepare my meal that evening and I did not give the message much thought.

In March 2020, I understood the severity of the message I had received in January. We were facing a global pandemic and some people did not handle it well by panic buying. I watched the news and saw that there was hardly any food, toilet roll or cleaning products left on the shelves of most supermarkets and local shops. My intuition was always right, this was famine. I made up carrier bags of cleaning materials, toilet rolls, hand sanitizer and latex gloves and I delivered them to people who were vulnerable and in need. I did not face the challenge of lack during the pandemic and my gratitude went up a notch. I was so very humbled by God's grace on my life. As I got to know myself more and know the love of God, life seemed so peaceful even in the midst of a global pandemic. Mike would return home every weekend and we grew closer than ever. We remained faithful and we were so grateful that we both did not suffer. We both continued with our chosen careers and we helped the less fortunate when we could. I managed to continue to support the service users and I kept them all safe and well. Some of the more vulnerable service users blamed me for not being able to go to visit their family and friends as they refused to believe that there was a national lock down. Most of the service users' would ask for a hug if they were upset but I had to keep on reminding them of the social distancing rules. The best I could do for the service users was to remain consistent with their support and offer more emotional support. One service user was approached by a landlord who persuaded her to leave her supported accommodation and to move in to one of his properties. He told the service user that she could get support for £5.00 a week. Being vulnerable, the service user left Pauline's supported accommodation. 6 weeks later, I received a call from the service user. She had attempted suicide due to the lack of support and poor living conditions and she begged me to please take her back. This was happening a lot within the supported accommodation. Some Service provider's were poaching vulnerable service users from there homes by telling them that they could live in their supported accommodation free of charge. What they failed to tell the service users was the poor conditions they would be living in and they also forgot to mention that there is not any support. Thankfully, I managed to keep all of the service users at Pauline's supported accommodation, safe and well looked after throughout the global pandemic.

A note from the Author

I faced many challenges during my time at Pauline's supported accommodation. I did all that I could to protect and support some of the most vulnerable adults. I also made sure that Pauline would be able to pay the bills on time as I always encouraged the service users to pay there service charges. A lot of the time, Pauline would be late with paying me my salary which would sometimes put me in the red with paying my household bills. I had to make changes by contacting companies to change my direct debit dates to a week later just so that I could pay my bills on time. I worked close with other professionals to support the service users but sometimes I felt as though I was alone. Pauline did not make my job any easier as I found her behaviour very challenging most times. At one point I almost walked away from the supported accommodation due to Pauline talking down to me for something she had failed to do and she put the blame on me but I remembered my vision and I also understood that I would be tested to build and shape my character and build resilience. Overall, I knew that I had stumbled on something very close to my heart. I knew that I had found a very narrow niche as I was dealing with service users who fell in the middle of care homes and supported accommodation. I loved the service users and they loved me in return. I accepted them for who they were and they all sensed my love and acceptance. I was always open and honest when I dealt with the service users and other professionals but I sometimes felt that I had been let down as some incidents I was left to deal with without anyone there to support me. I decided to do something about it. I met with one of my Zumba ladies who was also a business advisor. We talked over the telephone and came up with a plan on how I could create a model that supports the most vulnerable and creates a positive change in our world. My vision was getting bigger and clearer, I just needed to organise it in my mind and get it on paper.

As time passed, I took on more responsibilities and with responsibilities come bigger challenges. I used some of the tools I had learned from doing personal development and I often remembered the words of Mooji. I also found another spiritual teacher called Eckhart Tolle who teaches the same as Mooji but Eckhart explains the teachings different. I felt lighter and I carried peace with me wherever I went. I found that the teachings helped me to remain calm whilst faced with challenges and it seemed as though life was easier to understand. The service users' said that they could sense the peace that was around me and some said they felt safe and protected from being in my presence. Mike and I became more harmonious and our love grew deeper and stronger. I knew that this was the work of the Holy Spirit as His presence grew in me, it began to touch the lives of others.

In August 2020, Pauline and I had another disagreement. I was loosing the will to continue and I was finding it difficult to remain professional when I had any dealings with her. As I spoke with Mo most days, he could sense that I was becoming unhappy with working at Pauline's supported accommodation. Mo was also having challenges with his support worker and he suggested that we work together in partnership. Mo is a great landlord and service provider and I am a great housing support manager, together we would make a great team. I spoke with Mike about my challenges and he said that he could see that I was unhappy behind my smile. I made a decision on September 1st 2020 to end my contract. I gave Pauline one month's notice to find another contractor to run her supported accommodation.

CHAPTER 8

MOVING ON

Pauline and I had a few more disagreements but I was not taking it to heart as I only had a few days left before my contracted ended. I made a decision to tell the service users two days before 1ˢᵗ October. I made this decision as I did not want to leave the service users' with the sense of being abandoned. I gathered the service users' together in the communal living room and I watched their facial expressions as I told them that I was leaving. The service users did not look too concerned. They all said "We are not bothered because we are coming with you!" I explained that the property that I was moving to had no vacancies and I asked them to please stay at Pauline's supported accommodation. They protested saying that they do not want to stay if I am not going to be there. I was humbled and I felt the love but I did not want to be responsible for Pauline suffering a huge loss. I called Mo and told him the news. Mo asked me to persuade the service users to stay put. I spoke with the service users' again and they would not listen to what I was saying. One male service user said that his sister was looking for another supported accommodation for him as they were not happy with his living conditions. I spoke with the service users' sister to ask her if what I heard was true. The service users' sister who is called Anne said that she had been looking for another accommodation for a while. I told her that I wish her the best. Later on that day, Anne called me and asked if it was true that I was leaving. I told Anne that I would be leaving on 1ˢᵗ October. Anne asked if I could please find a room for her brother as he liked me and she knew he would be safe and well if I continued to meet his complex support needs. Another service user was looking to move to a supported accommodation as he also said that if I leave then he cannot stay. I was overwhelmed and I called Mo again. Mo and I spoke for a while as we worked out how we could provide accommodation for the service users who had made a decision to leave Pauline's supported accommodation. Mo decided to move his existing service users' to some of his other properties to make room for the ones who chose to follow me.

1st October arrived. My palms were sweaty and I felt uneasy as I left an inventory and the office keys on the desk in the office for Pauline. I checked in on the service users and said goodbye. Some of the service users had packed their bags and said they would join me on Monday 4th October.

I arrived at my new place of work and I felt a wave of relief wash over me. I reached for my phone to call Pauline's daughter as she was a reasonable lady and I had spoken with her in the past about I was finding it difficult to work with her mum. As I picked my phone up, Pauline rang. I answered my phone to Pauline who asked if everything was OK? I told her that I had left her office keys and an inventory in her office. Pauline protested and said that I should have given her a written notice. I answered by telling her that I had verbally told her that I was leaving and I reminded her of her own words when she told me that I was free to end the contract at any time. Why should I honour the contract by giving a written notice when Pauline found it OK to violate the said contract? This was not tit-for-tat, but I had grown tired of Pauline and I was loosing all respect for this lady. Pauline often said stuff and later would retreat or say she did not say it. She also made a decision and then changed it on a whim, this was very unstable, confusing and annoying, I was free at last. Pauline called me throughout the day to ask me questions about where things were and I repeated pointed Pauline to the inventory that I had left on her desk in her office. Mo stood by me and supported me by telling me that together we will make this happen. I set about making the house a home for the service users who were to arrive on Monday morning and the rest of the day I spent organising documents, support plans and menu's as I was getting ready to take some huge steps towards my dream. Mike called me and told me how proud of me he was and said we would celebrate my new beginnings tomorrow night.

Mike and I snuggled up on our sofa eating good food, listening to music and drinking beverages. This man has been my rock and strong support, I am truly humbled by his love and affection towards me.

Monday morning was an eventful one as some of the service users' moved in to the new property. The service users looked happy and began to settle in to their new home. Pauline's supported accommodation had 2 service users' left and so she had accused me of taking her service users but I know the truth as does Mo, Steve and the people I care about. Pauline had been my mentor for many years but that did not give her the right to speak down to me. I gave a months notice and left. The service users' decisions to follow me was not influenced by me in the slightest. I noticed after just a few days of being out of her supported accommodation how my life became harmonious, peaceful and stress free. I noticed that the service users laughed more and looked genuinely happy. I felt sad as this is not what I wanted but Pauline would not allow me to run the supported accommodation without her interfering and breathing down my neck. Pauline had mentored me to run supported accommodation and if she had just learned to work with me rather than against me then she would be reaping the benefits as I had her best interests at heart. I had put myself through courses to improve my performance, I supported the service users and I kept the company running smooth, the company did not make any financial losses so I could not understand why Pauline decided to make my life difficult. I decided to let go of the past and embrace the present. I feel it is important to write about my experiences from the heart. It was difficult to walk away from a lady who helped me but I also added huge value to Pauline and her project. Sometimes, Pauline made me question myself but not in a healthy way but I felt I was seeing myself under the eyes of criticism and it did not feel good. It was not only me who suffered Pauline's poor behaviour, almost everyone who had met Pauline through the supported accommodation said that she could be rude, abrupt and spoke down to others. I had a sense of honour and a sense of loyalty towards this lady and I guess I saw her through rose tinted glasses. I was sad to loose contact with Pauline but at the same time, I found her very difficult to be around. Pauline sent me an email saying that I should not have bitten the hand that fed me, she then blocked me on all of her social media accounts. I did not bite her hand. Pauline told me that she would stand back and allow me to be a contractor but she constantly undermined me and made my time difficult, so I walked away. That is not biting the hand hat fed me.

As time went by, I began to see huge improvements in the service users' well-being. I began setting up activities and creating a safe and warm environment. The service users' were enjoying the new stress free environment and Mo left me to run the supported accommodation but he always kept in touch and supported me. Mike said he saw a huge improvement in my well-being and was happy that I was finally happy in my role.

On December 14th my grandson came into the world. He stole my heart instantly as his mum and dad sent me photo's of his first few minutes on earth. Due to the Covid-19 restrictions, I was not able to visit the hospital but 5 days after he was born, I drove to Good Hope hospital to collect them and take both parents and my grandson home. My life is amazing!

CHAPTER 9

MEETING EMMA

January 2021 arrived. I sat and wrote down what I wanted to achieve this year. I knew I would benefit from having a physical mentor as I had gone on some of Eckhart Tolle's paid courses and brought his books as well as other books that helped me with my personal growth. I also continued to listen to Mooji and I found that listening to the 2 teacher's side by side, really helped me as they both spoke of the same message and I found both approaches worked well together for me.

Mike and I continued to grow as a couple and we continued to spend most weekends together and contacted each other daily throughout the week to uplift each other. Mike and I experienced love and harmony every day. I was blessed to have found such a kind, loving, compassionate, caring and respectful partner.

Mo and I worked very well as partners running the supported accommodations and the service users had settled in well.

As I wrote my vision for 2021, I contemplated what the year would bring. A few days later, I joined one of Bob Proctor's free 5 day challenges on a social media platform. To this day, I cannot recall how I came to find out about this challenge. I watched his first live teaching and his words seemed to be profound. I watched and listened to him talk about how the mind worked and I recall thinking that I must get back to being serious about creating my huge goal. In the group, some of the member's introduced themselves and wrote about why they decided to join Bob's 5 day challenge. I read some of the posts and encouraged the writers by sending a like or a love heart emoji. As I was getting in to my bed that night, I had an urge to share my story on the group. As soon as the idea came, I felt fear and I perceived a thought saying "Don't do it as people will judge you and mock you". I knew this was the voice of fear as my intuition does not speak in this way, as His tone is gentle and inspirational. I decided to get my phone out and I began to write my introduction post. I also added a photo of myself to the post and I pressed send. After about 5 minutes of sending the post, I received just over 30 likes and heart emojis. I decided to put my phone down and go to sleep.

When I woke up the next morning and after me giving thanks for another day, I picked up my phone. I opened my social media account and saw that I had hundreds of notifications. I opened the notifications and saw that I had over 600 likes and emojis and about 350 comments. As I read the comments and saw the love that I had received from the group members my heart was full of gratitude. I thanked the members in the group one by one to show my real appreciation. I received quite a few private messages from people in the group who told me of their current struggles and asked if I could help them with advice. I was overwhelmed but I decided to offer support and they all thanked me. Some people who saw my post were involved in network marketing and offered to send me information on the companies they worked in. There was one lady who messaged me and I could tell by her message that she was in deep emotional pain. I asked her if I could call her. She could not believe that I had responded to her message let alone offer her a telephone call to offer support. She quickly responded and before we knew it we were talking over the phone. An hour later when our call was over, I knew that I was going to be working with women who have been in personal development but had some how had the feeling of being emotionally stuck. I also spoke with people from over 10 different countries and I made some friendships with like-minded people who were also discovering the path to success.

A week after Bob's 5 day challenge, I received a message from a man who was in to net work marketing. Dan explained the company that he was involved in and I made a decision to join. The main reason for me joining was the mentorship that was involved. I also received a warm message from a PGI consultant. When I received this message, I looked at her profile picture and I felt as though I knew this lady. There was something about her that I could sense as genuine. She had warm eyes and was not coming across as wanting to sell me anything as most coaches I had come across in the past. This lady is called Emma and she was also doing a 5 day social media challenge on how to earn 6 figures in your business. I decided to join her group. As I attended Emma's free training sessions I intuitively knew that this lady would be my mentor. After the 5 days training, Emma reached out to me to ask if she could help me with my goal. I responded as I knew that I would benefit from investing in myself for a business mentor. I made the decision to join Emma's 12 week boot camp. As I went through the program, my vision became bigger and clearer and our relationship blossomed. Emma was and still is very professional and goes above and beyond for all of her clients. I told Emma about my past experiences and I told her that I had written a book back in 2012. Emma said she was humbled and she offered to show me how to be successful in my chosen field. As the boot camp drew to the last week, I did not want to loose Emma as a mentor and so when she called me with a special offer for me to invest in one of her high end packages, I quickly decided to invest more in myself. I have never looked back. Emma has some amazing qualities and she is authentic. I also remained in touch with the lady who I spoke to in January when I reached out to her from her message to me. She is called Molly. Molly lives in Canada with her husband and daughters. She is such a gentle soul. I also contacted my friend Stella who was one of my Zumba Fitness clients who was also a business advisor. I decided to merge us all together and this became the platform for creating a business model for how I can support vulnerable service users by creating unique packages. There was another lady who joined me with network marketing back in February who was also on the path to personal growth and I also invited her to brainstorm new idea's for my project, and before we knew it, we had developed a success masterclass. We got to work on how we could make the project work. I also had lots of advice from Emma. Mike and Mo were also very supportive with my vision and goal. I could see my vision getting bigger and I diligently followed the lead of my intuition. I also decided to make a huge investment in one of Eckhart's online courses where I would have lots of opportunities to see him live via Zoom calls and this made a huge difference in my spiritual growth. I had all the right people standing by me and supporting me too.

Following the promptings of the Holy Spirit and listening to His voice is a gift I will always be grateful for. I had to overcome some barriers to get to where I am today and no doubt, I will need to overcome more as I walk on my journey. The most important thing for me is to live in harmony and peace and answer my calling.

As I finish writing this account based on my true story, I would like to share some great news! Two weeks ago, I received a telephone call from the landlords who own the building of Pauline's supported accommodation. At first, I thought they called me accidentality as I had to communicate with them when I was a contractor at Pauline's supported accommodation. I sat and watched my mobile phone screen as the name appeared but I did not answer as I was sure he would disconnect the call. My phone continued to ring and so I decided to answer the call. The landlord called and explained that Pauline will not be running the supported accommodation after December 2021 and they asked me if I knew of anyone who would be willing to lease the property. My heart leaped and I replied, "I will". The landlord explained that Pauline was retiring and they wanted a smooth transition so that the building would not be left empty for a long period of time. We arranged to meet the following morning. I spoke with Mo and he said that he will support me. I also spoke with Mike who was so very supportive and who kept on telling me how proud he was of me. The following morning, I met with the landlords and we discussed how the lease would work. I spoke to Mo and asked him if we could do this together. Mo agreed. We arranged to meet at the property to have a viewing. Pauline has CCTV in and outside of the property. Mo and I arrived to view the property on Friday 5th November 2021. I did request a virtual viewing as I did not want Pauline to see me and Mo entering the supported accommodation as I knew it may upset her as she still blamed me for taking her service users last year but the landlords said that they would rather I had a physical feel of the property. Mo and I arrived at 10am and we were shown the specifics of the property. There was one service user who became a little confused when he saw me as I once supported him when I worked as a contractor back in 2019-2020. He immediately recognised me and began to tell me that he was hungry. The service user opened his arms to hug me but due to circumstances around covid-19 and the reasons as to why I was there, I politely made him aware that I cannot accept a hug but I spoke kind words to him and smiled. Whilst Mo and I were shown around the property, one of the landlords phone began to ring. He answered and I could hear Pauline's voice quite loud down the phone. The landlord looked at me and Mo with an apologetic smile and walked away to speak with Pauline over the phone. I could not hear what was said, but I could hear that she was not happy with what she saw on her CCTV. After about 10 minutes once Mo and I had viewed the property, we left and went about our daily business. I also had a business mentorship call with Emma at 11am and I told her my good news. Emma was giddy with joy and helped me to plan the way forward concerning how to offer the best service for the service users. Over the past couple of weeks, Emma has helped me get the results needed to help me on the path to success. Without this lady and those close to me, I could not have done this alone. I have met some amazing people in my life and I realise that we are all each others mentors and teachers. My grandson is one of my biggest teachers as he show me how children do not judge nor carry ill feelings. I find myself giddy when I see him and he sometimes looks at me as if he knows what I am thinking, maybe he does?

I look back at the last 10 years in awe. The building that was used to help me when I was broken, is the same building that has been handed to me on a plate for me to heal and give hope to the vulnerable through running a care and support service. I am humbled, extremely humbled.

A note from the Author - Final Word

My intention for writing my true life story, is to share some hard hitting truths and to bring healing to the readers who may feel that they cannot come out of their personal challenges. I hope to inspire people with a message of hope. I also wanted to share my overall view on how we can get trapped by the ones we once trusted and or loved. I have realised that people are not always what they seem to be. I believe that this is a life lesson and it can be learned by everyone. I learned this lesson from a very young age and still I managed to be fooled and trapped by a lady who I genuinely believed had my best interests at heart. Pauline appeared to be a wonderful, kind mentor and although I am grateful for all that she did for me I feel that it is important that I share with you, the wonderful and kind acts I also gave to her and her project as an act of gratitude, as this is not one sided.

I guess I saw Pauline's true colours one day when I told her that I had to leave her and her project as we could not work together, in my opinion, it was too soul destroying as she was a very challenging individual. Pauline told me that my vision will never stand without her. Pauline also showed me that she is not as mature as I once believed as I know that she has bad mouthed me to others by telling people that I took service users from her supported accommodation when I finally left in 2020. This is not true! When a person is genuinely loved by clients, some clients will follow that person as a sense of loyalty. The service users who decided to follow me had realised that I was willing and able to care and support them in their time of need. They did not see this in Pauline. Some of the service users told me that they could tell that Pauline and her husband did not care for them as I had and they went on to say that I made them feel special and loved. It has been just over a year since I left Pauline's supported accommodation and the service users' who followed me are flourishing and are coming on in leaps and bounds. I am not here to bad mouth Pauline or anyone, but this is my true story and I feel that I should be able to express myself freely. I want to conclude by saying that I have absolutely no hard feelings towards Pauline, her husband or her family. Pauline spoke to me like I was beneath her and did not show me real mentor qualities. I felt controlled and belittled by this lady even though she brought me gifts and some days she could be so warm and loving.

Life has shown me that we are our own creators as we have the power of choice and by using our power, we can create heaven or hell on earth. I have been fortunate to create a place of peace, joy and harmony but as you have read, it wasn't always so. My life quickly spiralled out of control and I was trapped in a dark hole, or so it seemed. I now know from experience that all things are truly possible and no one is beyond repair. I am looking forward to what the future holds for me and my loved ones. I am truly humbled by the Grace on my life and I want to share with the reader's of my true life experience what I offer to humanity to help my clients experience a life that is filled of acceptance, peace and happiness. I have become a mentor who loves, admires and wants only the very best for all of my clients. Peace and love be with you all. *xx*

What is the author doing now?

The service users' have structure and enjoy watching Netflix and Amazon Prime movies. They also enjoy going out to the zoo, sea-life centres and amusement centres such as Star City, twice a week as well as visiting the local park for a stroll where they often feed the swans and ducks with bread. The service users' also enjoy living in a comfortable, warm and safe home. I have fitted a video camera door bell for added security as a safeguarding measure, and they enjoy 3 meals a day, unlimited beverages and takeaways on the weekends. Some of the service users' are supported by Care Quality Commissioners (CQC) regulated support workers where their care and support needs are met. I am now living my dream. I also run an online mentorship program with clients who are serious about changing their results and I am proving to myself that I am a successful mentor with confidence.